ἈΡΙΣΤΟΦΑΝΟΥΣ   ARISTOPHANES'

Ὄρνιθες   *Birds*

A Dual Language Edition

Greek Text Edited (1907) by
F.W. Hall and W.M. Geldart

English Translation and Notes by
Ian Johnston

Edited by
Evan Hayes and Stephen Nimis

FAENUM PUBLISHING
OXFORD, OHIO

for Geoffrey (1974-1997)

οἵη περ φύλλων γενεὴ τοίη δὲ καὶ ἀνδρῶν.
φύλλα τὰ μέν τ᾽ ἄνεμος χαμάδις χέει, ἄλλα δέ θ᾽ ὕλη
τηλεθόωσα φύει, ἔαρος δ᾽ ἐπιγίγνεται ὥρη·
ὣς ἀνδρῶν γενεὴ ἣ μὲν φύει ἣ δ᾽ ἀπολήγει.

Generations of men are like the leaves.

In winter, winds blow them down to earth,
but then, when spring season comes again,
the budding wood grows more. And so with men:
one generation grows, another dies away. (*Iliad* 6)

TABLE OF CONTENTS

EDITORS' NOTE

This book presents the Greek text of Aristophanes' *Birds* with a facing English translation. The Greek text is that of F.W. Hall and W.M. Geldart, (1907), from the Oxford Classical Texts series, which is in the public domain and available as a pdf. This text has also been digitized by the Perseus Project (perseus.tufts.edu). The English translation and accompanying notes are those of Ian Johnston of Vancouver Island University, Nanaimo, BC. This translation is available freely online (records.viu.ca/~johnstoi/). We have reset both texts, making a number of very minor corrections, and placed them on opposing pages. This facing-page format will be useful to those wishing to read the English translation while looking at the Greek version, or vice versa.

HISTORICAL NOTE

The Birds was first produced at the drama festival in 414 BC, where it won second prize. At this period, during the Peloponnesian War, Athens was very powerful and confident, having just launched the expedition to Sicily, fully expecting to triumph in that venture and in the larger war.

ΌΡΝΙΘΕΣ

BIRDS

ΤΑ ΤΟΥ ΔΡΑΜΑΤΟΣ ΠΡΟΣΩΠΑ

ΠΙΣΘΕΤΑΙΡΟΣ

ΕΥΕΛΠΙΔΗΣ

ΘΕΡΑΠΩΝ

ΤΗΡΕΥΣ ἔποψ

ΦΟΙΝΙΚΟΠΤΕΡΟΣ*

ΤΑΩΣ*

ΕΠΟΨ Β*

ΚΑΤΩΦΑΓΑΣ ὄρνις*

ΧΟΡΟΣ ὀρνιθῶν

ΞΑΝΘΙΑΣ οἰκέτης*

ΜΑΝΟΔΩΡΟΣ οἰκέτης*

ΠΡΟΚΝΗ*

ΙΕΡΕΥΣ

ΠΟΙΗΤΞΣ

ΧΡΗΣΜΟΛΟΓΟΣ

ΜΕΤΩΝ γεωμέτρης

ΕΠΙΣΚΟΠΟΣ

ΨΗΦΙΣΜΑΤΟΠΩΛΗΣ

ΑΓΓΕΛΟΣ Α

ΑΓΓΕΛΟΣ Β

ΙΡΙΣ

ΚΗΡΥΞ Α

ΠΑΤΡΑΛΟΙΑΣ

ΚΙΝΗΣΙΑΣ διθυραμβοποιός

ΣΥΚΟΦΑΝΤΗΣ

ΠΡΟΜΗΘΕΥΣ

ΠΟΣΕΙΔΩΝ

ΗΡΑΚΛΗΣ

ΤΡΙΒΑΛΛΟΣ

ΒΑΣΙΛΕΙΑ*

ΚΗΡΥΞ Β

*κωφὸν πρόσωπον

DRAMATIS PERSONAE

PISTHETAIROS
a middle-aged Athenian

EUELPIDES
a middle-aged Athenian

SERVANT-BIRD
a slave serving Tereus, once a man

TEREUS
a hoopoe bird, once a man

FLAMINGO*

PEACOCK*

A SECOND HOOPOE*

GLUTTON-BIRD*
a fictitious species

CHORUS LEADER

CHORUS
of birds

XANTHIAS*
slave serving Pisthetairos

MANODOROS*
*slave serving Euelpides, also
called* MANES

PROCNE*
*a nightingale with a woman's body,
consort of Tereus*

PRIEST

POET

ORACLE MONGER
a collector and interpreter of oracles

METON
a land surveyor

COMMISSIONER OF
COLONIES
an Athenian official

STATUTE SELLER
man who sells laws

FIRST MESSENGER
a construction-worker bird

SECOND MESSENGER
a soldier bird

IRIS
messenger goddess, daughter of Zeus

FIRST HERALD
a bird

YOUNG MAN
*young Athenian who wants
to beat up his father*

CINESIAS
*a very bad dithyrambic poet and
singer*

SYCOPHANT
a common informer

PROMETHEUS
the Titan

POSEIDON
god of the sea, brother of Zeus

HERCULES
the legendary hero, now divine

TRIBALLIAN GOD
an uncouth barbarian god

PRINCESS*
a divine young lady

SECOND HERALD

* silent character

Ὄρνιθες

ΕΥΕΛΠΙΔΗΣ

ὀρθὴν κελεύεις, ᾗ τὸ δένδρον φαίνεται;

ΠΙΣΘΕΤΑΙΡΟΣ

διαρραγείης· ἥδε δ' αὖ κρώζει πάλιν.

ΕΥΕΛΠΙΔΗΣ

τί ὦ πόνηρ' ἄνω κάτω πλανύττομεν;
ἀπολούμεθ' ἄλλως τὴν ὁδὸν προφορουμένω.

ΠΙΣΘΕΤΑΙΡΟΣ

τὸ δ' ἐμὲ κορώνῃ πειθόμενον τὸν ἄθλιον   5
ὁδοῦ περιελθεῖν στάδια πλεῖν ἢ χίλια.

ΕΥΕΛΠΙΔΗΣ

τὸ δ' ἐμὲ κολοιῷ πειθόμενον τὸν δύσμορον
ἀποσποδῆσαι τοὺς ὄνυχας τῶν δακτύλων.

ΠΙΣΘΕΤΑΙΡΟΣ

ἀλλ' οὐδ' ὅπου γῆς ἐσμὲν οἶδ' ἔγωγ' ἔτι.

ΕΥΕΛΠΙΔΗΣ

ἐντευθενὶ τὴν πατρίδ' ἂν ἐξεύροις σύ που;   10

4

Birds

SCENE: A rugged, treed wilderness area up in the rocky hills. Enter Pisthetairos and Euelpides, both very tired. They are clambering down from the rocky heights towards the level stage. Pisthetairos has a crow perched on his arm or shoulder, and Euelpides has a jackdaw. Both Pisthetairos and Euelpides are carrying packs on their back. They are followed by two slaves carrying more bags. The slaves stay well out of the way until they get involved in the action later on.

EUELPIDES *[speaking to the bird he is carrying]*
    Are you telling us to keep going straight ahead?
    Over there by that tree?

PISTHETAIROS
                    Blast this bird—
    it's croaking for us to head back, go home.

EUELPIDES
    Why are we wandering up and down like this?
    You're such a fool—this endless weaving round
    will kill us both.

PISTHETAIROS
                 I must be an idiot
    to keep hiking on along these pathways,
    a hundred miles at least, and just because
    that's what this crow keeps telling me to do.

EUELPIDES
    What about me? My poor toe nails are thrashed.
    I've worn them out because I'm following
    what this jackdaw says.

PISTHETAIROS *[looking around]*
                  I have no idea
    where on earth we are.

EUELPIDES
              You mean from here
    you couldn't make it back to your place?   [10]

5

ΠΙΣΘΕΤΑΙΡΟΣ

οὐδ᾽ ἂν μὰ Δία γ᾽ ἐντεῦθεν Ἐξηκεστίδης.

ΕΥΕΛΠΙΔΗΣ

οἴμοι.

ΠΙΣΘΕΤΑΙΡΟΣ

σὺ μὲν ὦ τᾶν τὴν ὁδὸν ταύτην ἴθι.

ΕΥΕΛΠΙΔΗΣ

ἦ δεινὰ νὼ δέδρακεν οὐκ τῶν ὀρνέων,
ὁ πινακοπώλης φιλοκράτης μελαγχολῶν,
ὃς τώδ᾽ ἔφασκε νῷν φράσειν τὸν Τηρέα   15
τὸν ἔποφ᾽ ὃς ὄρνις ἐγένετ᾽ ἐκ τῶν ὀρνέων·
κἀπέδοτο τὸν μὲν Θαρρελείδου τουτονὶ
κολοιὸν ὀβολοῦ, τηνδεδὶ τριωβόλου.
τὼ δ᾽ οὐκ ἄρ᾽ ἤστην οὐδὲν ἄλλο πλὴν δάκνειν.
καὶ νῦν τί κέχηνας; ἔσθ᾽ ὅποι κατὰ τῶν πετρῶν   20
ἡμᾶς ἔτ᾽ ἔξεις. οὐ γάρ ἐστ᾽ ἐνταῦθά τις
ὁδός.

ΠΙΣΘΕΤΑΙΡΟΣ

οὐδὲ μὰ Δί᾽ ἐνταῦθά γ᾽ ἀτραπὸς οὐδαμοῦ.

ΕΥΕΛΠΙΔΗΣ

οὐδ᾽ ἡ κορώνη τῆς ὁδοῦ τι λέγει πέρι;

ΠΙΣΘΕΤΑΙΡΟΣ

οὐ ταὐτὰ κρώζει μὰ Δία νῦν τε καὶ τότε.

ΕΥΕΛΠΙΔΗΣ

τί δὴ λέγει περὶ τῆς ὁδοῦ;   25

ΠΙΣΘΕΤΑΙΡΟΣ

τί δ᾽ ἄλλο γ᾽ ἢ
βρύκουσ᾽ ἀπέδεσθαί φησί μου τοὺς δακτύλους;

PISTHETAIROS:
No way—not even Execestides
could manage that.[1]

EUELPIDES

We're in a real mess.

PISTHETAIROS

Well, you could try going along that pathway.

[The two men start exploring different paths down to opposite sides of the stage]

EUELPIDES

We two were conned by that Philokrates,
the crazy vendor in the marketplace
who sells his birds on trays. He claimed these two
would take us straight to Tereus the hoopoe,
a man who years ago became a bird.[2]
That's why we paid an obol for this one,
this jackdaw, son of Tharreleides.[3]
and three more for the crow. And then what?
The two know nothing, except how to bite.

[The jackdaw with Euelpides begins to get excited about something. Euelpides talks to the bird]

What's got your attention now? In those rocks?   [20]
You want to take us there? There's no way through.

PISTHETAIROS *[calling across the stage to Euelpides]*
By god, the same thing over here, no road.

EUELPIDES
What's your crow saying about the pathway?

PISTHETAIROS
By god, it's not cawing what it did before.

EUELPIDES *[shouting]*
But what's it saying about the road?

PISTHETAIROS

Nothing—
it's saying nothing, just keeps on croaking—
something about biting my fingers off.

Aristophanes

ΕΥΕΛΠΙΔΗΣ
οὐ δεινὸν οὖν δῆτ᾽ ἐστὶν ἡμᾶς δεομένους
ἐς κόρακας ἐλθεῖν καὶ παρεσκευασμένους
ἔπειτα μὴ ᾽ξευρεῖν δύνασθαι τὴν ὁδόν;
ἡμεῖς γάρ, ὦνδρες οἱ παρόντες ἐν λόγῳ,   30
νόσον νοσοῦμεν τὴν ἐναντίαν Σάκᾳ·
ὁ μὲν γὰρ ὢν οὐκ ἀστὸς ἐσβιάζεται,
ἡμεῖς δὲ φυλῇ καὶ γένει τιμώμενοι,
ἀστοὶ μετ᾽ ἀστῶν, οὐ σοβοῦντος οὐδενὸς
ἀνεπτόμεσθ᾽ ἐκ τῆς πατρίδος ἀμφοῖν ποδοῖν,   35
αὐτὴν μὲν οὐ μισοῦντ᾽ ἐκείνην τὴν πόλιν
τὸ μὴ οὐ μεγάλην εἶναι φύσει κεὐδαίμονα
καὶ πᾶσι κοινὴν ἐναποτεῖσαι χρήματα.
οἱ μὲν γὰρ οὖν τέττιγες ἕνα μῆν᾽ ἢ δύο
ἐπὶ τῶν κραδῶν ᾄδουσ᾽, Ἀθηναῖοι δ᾽ ἀεὶ   40
ἐπὶ τῶν δικῶν ᾄδουσι πάντα τὸν βίον.
διὰ ταῦτα τόνδε τὸν βάδον βαδίζομεν,
κανοῦν δ᾽ ἔχοντε καὶ χύτραν καὶ μυρρίνας
πλανώμεθα ζητοῦντε τόπον ἀπράγμονα,
ὅποι καθιδρυθέντε διαγενοίμεθ᾽ ἄν.   45
ὁ δὲ στόλος νῷν ἐστι παρὰ τὸν Τηρέα
τὸν ἔποπα, παρ᾽ ἐκείνου πυθέσθαι δεομένῳ,
εἴ που τοιαύτην εἶδε πόλιν ᾗ ᾽πέπτετο.

ΠΙΣΘΕΤΑΙΡΟΣ
οὗτος.

ΕΥΕΛΠΙΔΗΣ
τί ἔστιν;

ΠΙΣΘΕΤΑΙΡΟΣ
ἡ κορώνη μοι πάλαι
ἄνω τι φράζει.

ΕΥΕΛΠΙΔΗΣ
χὠ κολοιὸς οὑτοσὶ   50
ἄνω κέχηνεν ὡσπερεὶ δεικνύς τί μοι,
κοὐκ ἔσθ᾽ ὅπως οὐκ ἔστιν ἐνταῦθ᾽ ὄρνεα.
εἰσόμεθα δ᾽ αὐτίκ᾽, ἢν ποιήσωμεν ψόφον.

8

EUELPIDES *[addressing the audience]*
Don't you think it's really odd the two of us,
ready and eager to head off for the birds,[4]
just can't find the way. You see, we're not well.
All you men sitting there to hear our words,   [30]
we're ill with a disease, not like the one
which Sacas suffers,[5] no — the opposite.
He's no true citizen, yet nonetheless
he's pushing his way in by force, but we,
both honoured members of our tribe and clan,[6]
both citizens among you citizens,
with no one trying to drive us from the city,
have winged our way out of our native land
on our two feet. We don't hate the city
because we think it's not by nature great
and truly prosperous — open to all,
so they can spend their money paying fines.
Cicadas chirp up in the trees a while,
a month or two, but our Athenians   [40]
keep chirping over lawsuits all their lives.
That's why right now we've set off on this trip,
with all this stuff — basket, pot, and myrtle boughs.[7]
We're looking for a nice relaxing spot,
where we can settle down, live out our lives.
We're heading for Tereus, that hoopoe bird —
we'd like to know if in his flying around
he's seen a city like the one we want.

PISTHETAIROS
Hey!

EUELPIDES
    What?

PISTHETAIROS
          My crow keeps cawing upwards —
up there.

EUELPIDES
My jackdaw's looking up there, too,   [50]
as if it wants to show me something.
There must be birds around these rocks. I know —
let's make noise and then we'll see for sure.

ΠΙΣΘΕΤΑΙΡΟΣ
ἀλλ' οἶσθ' ὃ δρᾶσον; τῷ σκέλει θένε τὴν πέτραν.

ΕΥΕΛΠΙΔΗΣ
σὺ δὲ τῇ κεφαλῇ γ', ἵν' ᾖ διπλάσιος ὁ ψόφος.   55

ΠΙΣΘΕΤΑΙΡΟΣ
σὺ δ' οὖν λίθῳ κόψον λαβών.

ΕΥΕΛΠΙΔΗΣ
                                        πάνυ γ', εἰ δοκεῖ.
παῖ παῖ.

ΠΙΣΘΕΤΑΙΡΟΣ
τί λέγεις οὗτος; τὸν ἔποπα παῖ καλεῖς;
οὐκ ἀντὶ τοῦ παιδός σ' ἐχρῆν ἐποποῖ καλεῖν;

ΕΥΕΛΠΙΔΗΣ
ἐποποῖ. ποιήσεις ἔτι με κόπτειν αὖθις αὖ.
ἐποποῖ.   60

ΘΕΡΑΠΩΝ
                    τίνες οὗτοι; τίς ὁ βοῶν τὸν δεσπότην;

ΕΥΕΛΠΙΔΗΣ
Ἄπολλον ἀποτρόπαιε τοῦ χασμήματος.

ΘΕΡΑΠΩΝ
οἴμοι τάλας ὀρνιθοθήρα τουτωί.

ΕΥΕΛΠΙΔΗΣ
οὕτως τι δεινὸν οὐδὲ κάλλιον λέγειν.

ΘΕΡΑΠΩΝ
ἀπολεῖσθον.

10

PISTHETAIROS
You know what you should do? Kick that outcrop.

EUELPIDES
Why not use your head? There'd be twice the noise.

[Pisthetairos and Euelpides start climbing back up the rocky outcrops towards a door in the middle of the rocks]

PISTHETAIROS
Pick up a stone and then knock on the door.

EUELPIDES
All right. Here I go.

[Euelpides knocks very loudly on the door and calls out]

                  Hey, boy . . . boy!

PISTHETAIROS
What are you saying? Why call the hoopoe "boy"?
Don't say that—you should call out
[giving a bird call]
                 "hoopoe-ho."

EUELPIDES *[knocking on the door and calling again]*
Hoopoe-ho! . . . Should I knock again? . . . Hoopoe-ho!

SERVANT-BIRD *[inside]*
Who is it? Who's shouting for my master?   [60]

[The door opens and an actor-bird emerges. He has a huge beak which terrifies Euelpides and Pisthetairos. They fall back in fear, and the birds they have been carrying disappear]

EUELPIDES
My lord Apollo, save us! That gaping beak—

SERVANT-BIRD *[also frightened]*
Oh, oh, now we're in for it. You two men,
you're bird-catchers!

EUELPIDES
              Don't act so weird!
Can't you say something nice?

SERVANT-BIRD *[trying to scare them off]*
                 You two men will die!

ΕΥΕΛΠΙΔΗΣ

ἀλλ' οὐκ ἐσμὲν ἀνθρώπω.

ΘΕΡΑΠΩΝ

τί δαί;

ΕΥΕΛΠΙΔΗΣ

Ὑποδεδιὼς ἔγωγε Διβυκὸν ὄρνεον.   65

ΘΕΡΑΠΩΝ

οὐδὲν λέγεις.

ΕΥΕΛΠΙΔΗΣ

καὶ μὴν ἐροῦ τὰ πρὸς ποδῶν.

ΘΕΡΑΠΩΝ

ὁδὶ δὲ δὴ τίς ἐστιν ὄρνις; οὐκ ἐρεῖς;

ΠΙΣΘΕΤΑΙΡΟΣ

Ἐπικεχοδὼς ἔγωγε Φασιανικός.

ΕΥΕΛΠΙΔΗΣ

ἀτὰρ σὺ τί θηρίον ποτ' εἶ πρὸς τῶν θεῶν;

ΘΕΡΑΠΩΝ

ὄρνις ἔγωγε δοῦλος.

ΕΥΕΛΠΙΔΗΣ

ἡττήθης τινὸς   70
ἀλεκτρυόνος;

ΘΕΡΑΠΩΝ

οὐκ ἀλλ' ὅτε περ ὁ δεσπότης
ἔποψ ἐγένετο, τότε γενέσθαι μ' ηὔξατο
ὄρνιν, ἵν' ἀκόλουθον διάκονόν τ' ἔχῃ.

ΕΥΕΛΠΙΔΗΣ

δεῖται γὰρ ὄρνις καὶ διακόνου τινός;

ΘΕΡΑΠΩΝ

οὗτός γ', ἅτ' οἶμαι πρότερον ἄνθρωπός ποτ' ὤν,   75
τοτὲ μὲν ἐρᾷ φαγεῖν ἀφύας Φαληρικάς·
τρέχω 'π' ἀφύας λαβὼν ἐγὼ τὸ τρύβλιον.

12

EUELPIDES
But we're not men.

SERVANT-BIRD
What? What are you, then?

EUELPIDES
Well . . . I'm a chicken-shitter . . . a Libyan bird . . .

SERVANT-BIRD
That's rubbish.

EUELPIDES
No, it's not—I've just dropped my load—
down both my legs. Take a look.

SERVANT-BIRD
And this one here?
What kind of bird is he?
[to Pisthetairos]
Can you speak?

PISTHETAIROS
Me? . . . a crapper-fowl . . . from Phasis.

EUELPIDES
God knows what kind of animal you are!

SERVANT-BIRD
I'm a servant bird.

EUELPIDES
Beaten by some rooster   [70]
in a cock fight?

SERVANT-BIRD
No. It was my master—
when he became a hoopoe, well, I prayed
that I could turn into a bird. That way
he'd still have me to serve and wait on him.

EUELPIDES
Does a bird need his own butler bird?

SERVANT-BIRD
He does—I think it's got something to do
with the fact that earlier he was a man.
So if he wants to taste some fish from Phalerum,
I grab a plate and run off for sardines.

ἔτνους δ' ἐπιθυμεῖ, δεῖ τορύνης καὶ χύτρας·
τρέχω 'πὶ τορύνην.

ΕΥΕΛΠΙΔΗΣ

τροχίλος ὄρνις οὑτοσί.
οἶσθ' οὖν ὃ δρᾶσον ὦ τροχίλε; τὸν δεσπότην   80
ἡμῖν κάλεσον.

ΘΕΡΑΠΩΝ

ἀλλ' ἀρτίως νὴ τὸν Δία
εὕδει καταφαγὼν μύρτα καὶ σέρφους τινάς.

ΕΥΕΛΠΙΔΗΣ

ὅμως ἐπέγειρον αὐτόν.

ΘΕΡΑΠΩΝ

οἶδα μὲν σαφῶς
ὅτι ἀχθέσεται, σφῷν δ' αὐτὸν οὕνεκ' ἐπεγερῶ.

ΠΙΣΘΕΤΑΙΡΟΣ

κακῶς σύ γ' ἀπόλοι', ὥς μ' ἀπέκτεινας δέει.   85

ΕΥΕΛΠΙΔΗΣ

οἴμοι κακοδαίμων χὠ κολοιός μοἴχεται
ὑπὸ τοῦ δέους.

ΠΙΣΘΕΤΑΙΡΟΣ

ὦ δειλότατον σὺ θηρίον,
δείσας ἀφῆκας τὸν κολοιόν;

ΕΥΕΛΠΙΔΗΣ

εἰπέ μοι,
σὺ δὲ τὴν κορώνην οὐκ ἀφῆκας καταπεσών;

ΠΙΣΘΕΤΑΙΡΟΣ

μὰ Δί' οὐκ ἔγωγε.

ΕΥΕΛΠΙΔΗΣ

ποῦ γάρ ἐστ';

ΠΙΣΘΕΤΑΙΡΟΣ

ἀπέπτετο.   90

14

Birds

If he wants soup, we need pot and ladle,
so I dash off for the spoon.

EUELPIDES

A runner bird—
that's what you are. Well, my little runner,
do you know what we'd like to have you do?   [80]
Go call your master for us.

SERVANT-BIRD

But he's asleep—
for heaven's sake, his after-dinner snooze—
he's just had gnats and myrtle berries.

EUELPIDES
Wake him up anyway.

SERVANT-BIRD

I know for sure
he'll be annoyed, but I'll do it, just for you.

[Exit Servant-Bird back through the doors]

PISTHETAIROS
Damn that bird—he scared me half to death.

EUELPIDES
Bloody hell—he frightened off my bird!

PISTHETAIROS
You're such a coward—the worst there is.
Were you so scared you let that jackdaw go?

EUELPIDES
What about you? Didn't you collapse
and let your crow escape?

PISTHETAIROS

Not me, by god.

EUELPIDES
Where is it then?

PISTHETAIROS

It flew off on its own.   [90]

15

ΕΥΕΛΠΙΔΗΣ
οὐκ ἄρ’ ἀφῆκας; ὦγάθ’ ὡς ἀνδρεῖος εἶ.

ΤΗΡΕΥΣ
ἄνοιγε τὴν ὕλην, ἵν’ ἐξέλθω ποτέ.

ΕΥΕΛΠΙΔΗΣ
ὦ Ἡράκλεις τουτὶ τί ποτ’ ἐστὶ τὸ θηρίον;
τίς ἡ πτέρωσις; τίς ὁ τρόπος τῆς τριλοφίας;

ΤΗΡΕΥΣ
τίνες εἰσί μ’ οἱ ζητοῦντες;   95

ΕΥΕΛΠΙΔΗΣ
                                        οἱ δώδεκα θεοὶ
εἴξασιν ἐπιτρῦψαί σε.

ΤΗΡΕΥΣ
                        μῶν με σκώπτετον
ὁρῶντε τὴν πτέρωσιν; ἦν γὰρ ὦ ξένοι
ἄνθρωπος.

ΕΥΕΛΠΙΔΗΣ
                οὐ σοῦ καταγελῶμεν.

ΤΗΡΕΥΣ
                                        ἀλλὰ τοῦ;

ΕΥΕΛΠΙΔΗΣ
τὸ ῥάμφος ἡμῖν σου γέλοιον φαίνεται.

ΤΗΡΕΥΣ
τοιαῦτα μέντοι Σοφοκλέης λυμαίνεται   100
ἐν ταῖς τραγῳδίαισιν ἐμὲ τὸν Τηρέα.

ΕΥΕΛΠΙΔΗΣ
Τηρεὺς γὰρ εἶ σύ; πότερον ὄρνις ἢ ταῶς;

ΤΗΡΕΥΣ
ὄρνις ἔγωγε.

ΕΥΕΛΠΙΔΗΣ
                κᾆτά σοι ποῦ τὰ πτερά;

16

EUELPIDES
> You didn't let go? What a valiant man!

TEREUS *[from inside, speaking in a grand style]*
> Throw open this wood, so I may issue forth.

[The doors open. Enter Tereus, a hoopoe bird, with feathers on his head and wings but none on his body. He struts and speaks with a ridiculously affected confidence. Euelpides and Pisthetairos are greatly amused at his appearance]

EUELPIDES
> O Hercules, what kind of beast is this?
> What's that plumage? What sort of triple crest?

TEREUS
> Who are the persons here who seek me out?

EUELPIDES
> The twelve gods, it seems, have worked you over.[8]

TEREUS
> Does seeing my feathers make you scoff at me?
> Strangers, I was once upon a time a man.

EUELPIDES
> It's not you we're laughing at.

TEREUS
>   Then what is it?

EUELPIDES
> It's your beak—to us it looks quite funny.

TEREUS
> It's how Sophocles distorts Tereus—   [100]
> that's me—in his tragedies.

EUELPIDES
>   You're Tereus?
> Are you a peacock or a bird?[9]

TEREUS
>   I am a bird.

EUELPIDES
> Then where are all your feathers?

ΤΗΡΕΥΣ
ἐξερρύηκε.

ΕΥΕΛΠΙΔΗΣ
πότερον ὑπὸ νόσου τινός;

ΤΗΡΕΥΣ
οὔκ, ἀλλὰ τὸν χειμῶνα πάντα τὤρνεα   105
πτερορρυεῖ τε καὖθις ἕτερα φύομεν.
ἀλλ' εἴπατόν μοι σφὼ τίν' ἐστόν;

ΕΥΕΛΠΙΔΗΣ
                          νώ; βροτώ.

ΤΗΡΕΥΣ
ποδαπὼ τὸ γένος;

ΕΥΕΛΠΙΔΗΣ
                          ὅθεν αἱ τριήρεις αἱ καλαί.

ΤΗΡΕΥΣ
μῶν ἡλιαστά;

ΕΥΕΛΠΙΔΗΣ
                          μἀλλὰ θατέρου τρόπου,
ἀπηλιαστά.

ΤΗΡΕΥΣ
                          σπείρεται γὰρ τοῦτ' ἐκεῖ   110
τὸ σπέρμ';

ΕΥΕΛΠΙΔΗΣ
                          ὀλίγον ζητῶν ἂν ἐξ ἀγροῦ λάβοις.

ΤΗΡΕΥΣ
πράγους δὲ δὴ τοῦ δεομένω δεῦρ' ἤλθετον;

ΕΥΕΛΠΙΔΗΣ
σοὶ ξυγγενέσθαι βουλομένω.

ΤΗΡΕΥΣ
                          τίνος πέρι;

18

TEREUS

They've fallen off.

EUELPIDES

Have you got some disease?

TEREUS

No, it's not that.
In winter time all birds shed their feathers,
then new ones grow again. But tell me this—
who are the two of you?

EUELPIDES

Us? We're human beings.

TEREUS

From what race were you born?

EUELPIDES

Our origin?
In Athens—which makes the finest warships.

TEREUS

Ah, so you're jury-men, are you?

EUELPIDES

No, no.
We're different—we keep away from juries.

TEREUS

Does that seedling flourish in those parts?   [110]

EUELPIDES

If you go searching in the countryside,
you'll find a few.

TEREUS

So why have you come here?
What do you need?

EUELPIDES

To talk to you.

TEREUS

What for?

ΕΥΕΛΠΙΔΗΣ
ὅτι πρῶτα μὲν ἦσθ᾽ ἄνθρωπος ὥσπερ νὼ ποτέ,
κἀργύριον ὠφείλησας ὥσπερ νὼ ποτέ,   115
κοὐκ ἀποδιδοὺς ἔχαιρες ὥσπερ νὼ ποτέ·
εἶτ᾽ αὖθις ὀρνίθων μεταλλάξας φύσιν
καὶ γῆν ἐπέπτου καὶ θάλατταν ἐν κύκλῳ,
καὶ πάνθ᾽ ὅσαπερ ἄνθρωπος ὅσα τ᾽ ὄρνις φρονεῖς·
ταῦτ᾽ οὖν ἱκέται νὼ πρὸς σὲ δεῦρ᾽ ἀφίγμεθα,   120
εἴ τινα πόλιν φράσειας ἡμῖν εὔερον
ὥσπερ σισύραν ἐγκατακλινῆναι μαλθακήν.

ΤΗΡΕΥΣ
ἔπειτα μείζω τῶν Κραναῶν ζητεῖς πόλιν;

ΕΥΕΛΠΙΔΗΣ
μείζω μὲν οὐδέν, προσφορωτέραν δὲ νῷν.

ΤΗΡΕΥΣ
ἀριστοκρατεῖσθαι δῆλος εἶ ζητῶν.   125

ΕΥΕΛΠΙΔΗΣ
                                        ἐγώ;
ἥκιστα· καὶ γὰρ τὸν Σκελίου βδελύττομαι.

ΤΗΡΕΥΣ
ποίαν τιν᾽ οὖν ἥδιστ᾽ ἂν οἰκοῖτ᾽ ἂν πόλιν;

ΕΥΕΛΠΙΔΗΣ
ὅπου τὰ μέγιστα πράγματ᾽ εἴη τοιάδε·
ἐπὶ τὴν θύραν μου πρῴ τις ἐλθὼν τῶν φίλων
λέγοι ταδί· ᾽πρὸς τοῦ Διὸς τοὐλυμπίου   130
ὅπως παρέσει μοι καὶ σὺ καὶ τὰ παιδία
λουσάμενα πρῴ· μέλλω γὰρ ἑστιᾶν γάμους·
καὶ μηδαμῶς ἄλλως ποιήσῃς· εἰ δὲ μή,
μή μοι τότε γ᾽ ἔλθῃς, ὅταν ἐγὼ πράττω κακῶς.᾽

ΤΗΡΕΥΣ
νὴ Δία ταλαιπώρων γε πραγμάτων ἐρᾷς.   135
τί δαὶ σύ;

20

EUELPIDES

    Well, you were once a man, as we are now.
    You owed people money, as we do now.
    You loved to skip the debt, as we do now.
    Then you changed your nature, became a bird.
    You fly in circles over land and sea.
    You've learned whatever's known to birds and men.
    That's why we've come as suppliants to you,   [120]
    to ask if you can tell us of some town,
    where life is sheepskin soft, where we can sleep.

TEREUS

    Are you looking for a mighty city,
    more powerful than what Cranaus built?[10]

EUELPIDES

    Not one more powerful, no. What we want
    is one which better suits the two of us.

TEREUS

    You clearly want an aristocracy.

EUELPIDES

    Me? No, not at all. The son of Scellias
    is someone I detest.[11]

TEREUS

                            All right, then,
    What kind of city would you like to live in?

EUELPIDES

    I'd like a city where my biggest problem
    would be something like this—in the morning
    a friend comes to my door and says to me,
    "In the name of Olympian Zeus, take a bath,   [130]
    an early one, you and your children,
    then come to my place for the wedding feast
    I'm putting on. Don't disappoint me now.
    If you do, then don't come looking for me
    when my affairs get difficult for me."[12]

TEREUS

    By heaven, you poor man, you do love trouble.
    What about you?

ΠΙΣΘΕΤΑΙΡΟΣ

    τοιούτων ἐρῶ κἀγώ.

ΤΗΡΕΥΣ

                τίνων;

ΠΙΣΘΕΤΑΙΡΟΣ

ὅπου ξυναντῶν μοι ταδί τις μέμψεται
ὥσπερ ἀδικηθεὶς παιδὸς ὡραίου πατήρ·
'καλῶς γέ μου τὸν υἱὸν ὦ Στιλβωνίδη
εὑρὼν ἀπιόντ' ἀπὸ γυμνασίου λελουμένον   140
οὐκ ἔκυσας, οὐ προσεῖπας, οὐ προσηγάγου,
οὐκ ὠρχιπέδισας, ὢν ἐμοὶ πατρικὸς φίλος.'

ΤΗΡΕΥΣ

ὦ δειλακρίων σὺ τῶν κακῶν οἵων ἐρᾷς.
ἀτὰρ ἔστι γ' ὁποίαν λέγετον εὐδαίμων πόλις
παρὰ τὴν ἐρυθρὰν θάλατταν.   145

ΕΥΕΛΠΙΔΗΣ

                οἴμοι μηδαμῶς
ἡμῖν παρὰ τὴν θάλατταν, ἵν' ἀνακύψεται
κλητῆρ' ἄγουσ' ἕωθεν ἡ Σαλαμινία.
Ἑλληνικὴν δὲ πόλιν ἔχεις ἡμῖν φράσαι;

ΤΗΡΕΥΣ

τί οὐ τὸν Ἠλεῖον Λέπρεον οἰκίζετον
ἐλθόνθ';

ΕΥΕΛΠΙΔΗΣ

         ὁτιὴ νὴ τοὺς θεοὺς ὅσ' οὐκ ἰδὼν   150
βδελύττομαι τὸν Λέπρεον ἀπὸ Μελανθίου.

ΤΗΡΕΥΣ

ἀλλ' εἰσὶν ἕτεροι τῆς Λοκρίδος Ὀπούντιοι,
ἵνα χρὴ κατοικεῖν.

ΕΥΕΛΠΙΔΗΣ

                ἀλλ' ἔγωγ' Ὀπούντιος
οὐκ ἂν γενοίμην ἐπὶ ταλάντῳ χρυσίου.

PISTHETAIROS
>   I'd like the same.

TEREUS
>   Like what?

PISTHETAIROS
> To have the father of some handsome lad
> come up to me, as if I'd done him wrong,
> and tell me off with some complaint like this—
> "A fine thing there between you and my son,   [140]
> you old spark. You met him coming back
> from the gymnasium, after his bath—
> you didn't kiss or greet him with a hug,
> or even try tickling his testicles—
> yet you're a friend of mine, his father."

TEREUS
> How you yearn for problems, you unhappy man.
> There is a happy city by the sea,
> the Red Sea, just like the one you mention.¹³

EUELPIDES
> No, no. Not by the sea! That's not for us,
> not where that ship Salamia can show up
> with some man on board to serve a summons
> early in the morning.¹⁴ What about Greece?
> Can you tell us of some city there?

TEREUS
> Why not go and settle down in Elis—
> in Lepreus?

EUELPIDES
>   In Leprous? By the gods,
> I hate the place—although I've never seen it—   [150]
> it's all Melanthius' fault.¹⁵

TEREUS
>   You could go
> to the Opuntians—they're in Locris—
> you might settle there.

EUELPIDES
>   Be Opuntius—
> no way, not for a talent's weight in gold.¹⁶

οὗτος δὲ δὴ τίς ἔσθ᾽ ὁ μετ᾽ ὀρνίθων βίος;   155
σὺ γὰρ οἶσθ᾽ ἀκριβῶς.

ΤΗΡΕΥΣ
    οὐκ ἄχαρις ἐς τὴν τριβήν·
οὗ πρῶτα μὲν δεῖ ζῆν ἄνευ βαλλαντίου.

ΕΥΕΛΠΙΔΗΣ
πολλήν γ᾽ ἀφεῖλες τοῦ βίου κιβδηλίαν.

ΤΗΡΕΥΣ
νεμόμεσθα δ᾽ ἐν κήποις τὰ λευκὰ σήσαμα
καὶ μύρτα καὶ μήκωνα καὶ σισύμβρια.   160

ΕΥΕΛΠΙΔΗΣ
ὑμεῖς μὲν ἄρα ζῆτε νυμφίων βίον.

ΠΙΣΘΕΤΑΙΡΟΣ
φεῦ φεῦ·
ἦ μέγ᾽ ἐνορῶ βούλευμ᾽ ἐν ὀρνίθων γένει,
καὶ δύναμιν ἣ γένοιτ᾽ ἄν, εἰ πίθοισθέ μοι.

ΤΗΡΕΥΣ
τί σοι πιθώμεσθ᾽;

ΠΙΣΘΕΤΑΙΡΟΣ
    ὅ τι πίθησθε; πρῶτα μὲν
μὴ περιπέτεσθε πανταχῇ κεχηνότες·   165
ὡς τοῦτ᾽ ἄτιμον τοὔργον ἐστίν. αὐτίκα
ἐκεῖ παρ᾽ ἡμῖν τοὺς πετομένους ἢν ἔρῃ,
'τίς ὄρνις οὗτος;' ὁ Τελέας ἐρεῖ ταδί·
'ἄνθρωπος ὄρνις ἀστάθμητος πετόμενος,
ἀτέκμαρτος, οὐδὲν οὐδέποτ᾽ ἐν ταὐτῷ μένων.'   170

ΤΗΡΕΥΣ
νὴ τὸν Διόνυσον εὖ γε μωμᾷ ταυταγί.
τί ἂν οὖν ποιοῖμεν;

ΠΙΣΘΕΤΑΙΡΟΣ
    οἰκίσατε μίαν πόλιν.

ΤΗΡΕΥΣ
ποίαν δ᾽ ἂν οἰκίσαιμεν ὄρνιθες πόλιν;

But what's it like here, living with the birds?
You must know it well.

TEREUS

                It's not unpleasant.
First of all, you have to live without a purse.

EUELPIDES

So you're rid of one great source of fraud in life.

TEREUS

In the gardens we enjoy white sesame,   [160]
the myrtles, mint, and poppies.

EUELPIDES

                So you live
just like newly-weds.

PISTHETAIROS

                That's it! I've got it!
I see a great plan for this race of birds—
and power, too, if you'll trust what I say.

TEREUS

What do you want to get us all to do?

PISTHETAIROS

What should you be convinced to do? Well, first,
don't just fly about in all directions,
your beaks wide open—that makes you despised.
With us, you see, if you spoke of men
who always flit about and if you asked,
"Who's that Teleas" someone would respond,
"The man's a bird—he's unreliable,
flighty, vague, never stays in one place long."¹⁷   [170]

TEREUS

By Dionysus, that's a valid point—
the criticism's fair. What should we do?

PISTHETAIROS

Settle down together in one city.

TEREUS

What sort of city could we birds set up?

ΠΙΣΘΕΤΑΙΡΟΣ
ἄληθες; ὦ σκαιότατον εἰρηκὼς ἔπος,
βλέψον κάτω.   175

ΤΗΡΕΥΣ
καὶ δὴ βλέπω.

ΠΙΣΘΕΤΑΙΡΟΣ
βλέπε νῦν ἄνω.

ΤΗΡΕΥΣ
βλέπω.

ΠΙΣΘΕΤΑΙΡΟΣ
περίαγε τὸν τράχηλον.

ΤΗΡΕΥΣ
νὴ Δία
ἀπολαύσομαί τί γ᾽, εἰ διαστραφήσομαι.

ΠΙΣΘΕΤΑΙΡΟΣ
εἶδές τι;

ΤΗΡΕΥΣ
τὰς νεφέλας γε καὶ τὸν οὐρανόν.

ΠΙΣΘΕΤΑΙΡΟΣ
οὐχ οὗτος οὖν δήπου ᾽στὶν ὀρνίθων πόλος;

ΤΗΡΕΥΣ
πόλος; τίνα τρόπον;

ΠΙΣΘΕΤΑΙΡΟΣ
ὥσπερ ἂν εἴποι τις τόπος.   180
ὅτι δὲ πολεῖται τοῦτο καὶ διέρχεται
ἅπαντα διὰ τούτου, καλεῖται νῦν πόλος.
ἢν δ᾽ οἰκίσητε τοῦτο καὶ φάρξηθ᾽ ἅπαξ,
ἐκ τοῦ πόλου τούτου κεκλήσεται πόλις.
ὥστ᾽ ἄρξετ᾽ ἀνθρώπων μὲν ὥσπερ παρνόπων,   185
τοὺς δ᾽ αὖ θεοὺς ἀπολεῖτε λιμῷ Μηλίῳ.

ΤΗΡΕΥΣ
πῶς;

26

PISTHETAIROS
Why ask that? What a stupid thing to say!
Look down.

TEREUS
        All right.

PISTHETAIROS
             Now look up.

TEREUS
                  I'm looking up.

PISTHETAIROS
Turn your head round to the side.

TEREUS
                  By Zeus,
this'll do me good, if I twist off my neck.

PISTHETAIROS
What do you see?

TEREUS
           Clouds and sky.

PISTHETAIROS
               Well, then,
isn't this a staging area for birds?

TEREUS
A staging area? How come it's that?

PISTHETAIROS
You might say it's a location for them —   [180]
there's lots of business here, but everything
keeps moving through this zone, so it's now called
a staging place. But if you settled here,
fortified it, and fenced it off with walls,
this staging area could become your state.
Then you'd rule all men as if they're locusts
and annihilate the gods with famine,
just like in Melos.[18]

TEREUS
           How'd we manage that?

ΠΙΣΘΕΤΑΙΡΟΣ
    ἐν μέσῳ δήπουθεν ἀήρ ἐστι γῆς.
  εἶθ' ὥσπερ ἡμεῖς, ἢν ἰέναι βουλώμεθα
  Πυθώδε, Βοιωτοὺς δίοδον αἰτούμεθα,
  οὕτως, ὅταν θύσωσιν ἄνθρωποι θεοῖς,   190
  ἢν μὴ φόρον φέρωσιν οἱ ὑμῖν οἱ θεοί,
  διὰ τῆς πόλεως τῆς ἀλλοτρίας καὶ τοῦ χάους
  τῶν μηρίων τὴν κνῖσαν οὐ διαφρήσετε.

ΤΗΡΕΥΣ
  ἰοὺ ἰού·
  μὰ γῆν μὰ παγίδας μὰ νεφέλας μὰ δίκτυα,
  μὴ 'γὼ νόημα κομψότερον ἤκουσά πω·   195
  ὥστ' ἂν κατοικίζοιμι μετὰ σοῦ τὴν πόλιν,
  εἰ ξυνδοκοίη τοῖσιν ἄλλοις ὀρνέοις.

ΠΙΣΘΕΤΑΙΡΟΣ
  τίς ἂν οὖν τὸ πρᾶγμ' αὐτοῖς διηγήσαιτο;

ΤΗΡΕΥΣ
              σύ.
  ἐγὼ γὰρ αὐτοὺς βαρβάρους ὄντας πρὸ τοῦ
  ἐδίδαξα τὴν φωνήν, ξυνὼν πολὺν χρόνον.   200

ΠΙΣΘΕΤΑΙΡΟΣ
  πῶς δῆτ' ἂν αὐτοὺς ξυγκαλέσειας;

ΤΗΡΕΥΣ
            ῥᾳδίως.
  δευρὶ γὰρ ἐσβὰς αὐτίκα μάλ' ἐς τὴν λόχμην,
  ἔπειτ' ἀνεγείρας τὴν ἐμὴν ἀηδόνα,
  καλοῦμεν αὐτούς· οἱ δὲ νῷν τοῦ φθέγματος
  ἐάνπερ ἐπακούσωσι θεύσονται δρόμῳ.   205

ΠΙΣΘΕΤΑΙΡΟΣ
  ὦ φίλτατ' ὀρνίθων σὺ μή νυν ἔσταθι·
  ἀλλ' ἀντιβολῶ σ' ἄγ' ὡς τάχιστ' ἐς τὴν λόχμην
  ἔσβαινε κἀνέγειρε τὴν ἀηδόνα.

ΤΗΡΕΥΣ
    ἄγε σύννομέ μοι παῦσαι μὲν ὕπνου,
    λῦσον δὲ νόμους ἱερῶν ὕμνων,   210

PISTHETAIROS

    Look, between earth and heaven there's the air.
    Now, with us, when we want to go to Delphi,
    we have to ask permission to pass through
    from the Boeotians. You should do the same.
    When men sacrifice, make gods pay you cash.   [190]
    If not, you don't grant them rights of passage.
    You'll stop the smell of roasting thigh bones
    moving through an empty space and city
    which don't belong to them.

TEREUS

                         Wow!!! Yippee!!
    By earth, snares, traps, nets, what a marvellous scheme!
    I've never heard a neater plan! So now,
    with your help, I'm going to found a city,
    if other birds agree.

PISTHETAIROS

                    The other birds?
    Who's going to lay this business out to them?

TEREUS

    You can do it. I've taught them how to speak.   [200]
    Before I came, they could only twitter,
    but I've been with them here a long, long time.

PISTHETAIROS

    How do you call to bring them all together?

TEREUS

    Easy. I'll step inside my thicket here,
    and wake my nightingale. Then we'll both call.
    Once they hear our voices they'll come running.

PISTHETAIROS

    O, you darling bird, now don't just stand there —
    not when I'm begging you to go right now,
    get in your thicket, wake your nightingale.

[Tereus goes back through the doors] [19]

TEREUS *[singing]*

    Come my queen, don't sleep so long,
    pour forth the sound of sacred song —   [210]
    lament once more through lips divine

οὓς διὰ θείου στόματος θρηνεῖς
τὸν ἐμὸν καὶ σὸν πολύδακρυν Ἴτυν·
ἐλελιζομένης δ᾿ ἱεροῖς μέλεσιν
γένυος ξουθῆς
καθαρὰ χωρεῖ διὰ φυλλοκόμου 215
μίλακος ἠχὼ πρὸς Διὸς ἕδρας,
ἵν᾿ ὁ χρυσοκόμας Φοῖβος ἀκούων
τοῖς σοῖς ἐλέγοις ἀντιψάλλων
ἐλεφαντόδετον φόρμιγγα θεῶν
ἵστησι χορούς· διὰ δ᾿ ἀθανάτων 220
στομάτων χωρεῖ ξύμφωνος ὁμοῦ
θεία μακάρων ὀλολυγή.

ΕΥΕΛΠΙΔΗΣ
ὦ Ζεῦ βασιλεῦ τοῦ φθέγματος τοὐρνιθίου·
οἷον κατεμελίτωσε τὴν λόχμην ὅλην.

ΠΙΣΘΕΤΑΙΡΟΣ
οὗτος.

ΕΥΕΛΠΙΔΗΣ
τί ἔστιν;

ΠΙΣΘΕΤΑΙΡΟΣ
οὐ σιωπήσει;

ΠΙΣΘΕΤΑΙΡΟΣ
τί δαί; 225

ΠΙΣΘΕΤΑΙΡΟΣ
οὔποψ μελῳδεῖν αὖ παρασκευάζεται.

ΤΗΡΕΥΣ
ἐποποῖ ποποποποποποῖ,
ἰὼ ἰὼ ἰτὼ ἰτὼ ἰτὼ ἰτώ,
ἴτω τις ὧδε τῶν ἐμῶν ὁμοπτέρων·

30

for Itys, your dead child and mine,
the one we've cried for all this time.[20]

Sing out your music's liquid trill
in that vibrato voice—the thrill
which echoes in those purest tones
through leafy haunts of yew trees roams
and rises up to Zeus' throne.

Apollo with the golden hair
sits listening to your music there—
and in response he plucks his string—
his lyre of ivory then brings
the gods themselves to dance and sing.

Then from gods' mouths in harmony   [220]
come sounds of sacred melody.

[A flute starts playing within, in imitation of the nightingale's song. The melody continues for a few moments]

EUELPIDES
By lord Zeus, that little birdie's got a voice!
She pours her honey all through that thicket!

PISTHETAIROS
Hey!

EUELPIDES
       What?

PISTHETAIROS
            Shut up.

EUELPIDES
                Why?

PISTHETAIROS
                    That hoopoe bird—
he's all set to sing another song.

TEREUS *[issuing a bird call to all the birds. His song or chant is accompanied by the flute indicating the nightingale's song]*
Epo-popo-popo-popo-popoi,
Io, io, ito, ito, ito, ito.

Come here to me,
all you with feathers just like mine,   [230]

Aristophanes

ὅσοι τ᾽ εὐσπόρους ἀγροίκων γύας   230
νέμεσθε, φῦλα μυρία κριθοτράγων
σπερμολόγων τε γένη
ταχὺ πετόμενα, μαλθακὴν ἱέντα γῆρυν·
ὅσα τ᾽ ἐν ἄλοκι θαμὰ
βῶλον ἀμφιτιττυβίζεθ᾽ ὧδε λεπτὸν   235
ἡδομένα φωνᾷ·
τιὸ τιὸ τιὸ τιὸ τιὸ τιὸ τιό.

ὅσα θ᾽ ὑμῶν κατὰ κήπους ἐπὶ κισσοῦ
κλάδεσι νομὸν ἔχει,
τά τε κατ᾽ ὄρεα τά τε κοτινοτράγα τά τε κομαροφάγα,   240
ἀνύσατε πετόμενα πρὸς ἐμὰν αὐδάν·
τριοτὸ τριοτὸ τοτοβρίξ·

οἵ θ᾽ ἑλείας παρ᾽ αὐλῶνας ὀξυστόμους
ἐμπίδας κάπτεθ᾽, ὅσα τ᾽ εὐδρόσους γῆς τόπους   245
ἔχετε λειμῶνά τ᾽ ἐρόεντα Μαραθῶνος, ὄρνις
πτερυγοποίκιλός τ᾽ ἀτταγᾶς ἀτταγᾶς.

ὧν τ᾽ ἐπὶ πόντιον οἶδμα θαλάσσης   250
φῦλα μετ᾽ ἀλκυόνεσσι ποτῆται,
δεῦρ᾽ ἴτε πευσόμενοι τὰ νεώτερα,
πάντα γὰρ ἐνθάδε φῦλ᾽ ἀθροΐζομεν
οἰωνῶν ταναοδείρων.
ἥκει γὰρ τις δριμὺς πρέσβυς   255
καινὸς γνώμην
καινῶν τ᾽ ἔργων ἐγχειρητής.
ἀλλ᾽ ἴτ᾽ ἐς λόγους ἅπαντα,

32

all you who live in country fields
fresh-ploughed, still full of seed,
and all you thousand tribes
who munch on barley corn
who gather up the grain,
and fly at such a speed
and utter your sweet cries,
all you who in the furrows there
twitter on the turned-up earth,
and sweetly sing
tio tio tio tio tio tio tio tio—

All those of you
who like to scavenge food
from garden ivy shoots,   [240]
all you in the hills up there
who eat from olive and arbutus trees.
come here as quickly as you can,
fly here in answer to this call—
trio-to trio-to toto-brix!

And every one of you
in low-lying marshy ground
who snap sharp-biting gnats,
by regions of well-watered land,
and lovely fields of Marathon,
all you variously coloured birds,
godwits and francolins—
I'm calling you.

You flocks who fly across the seas   [250]
across the waves with halcyons
come here to learn the news.
We're all assembling here,
all tribes of long-neck birds.
A shrewd old man's arrived—
he's here with a new plan,
a man of enterprise,
all set to improvise.
So gather all of you
to hear his words.

δεῦρο δεῦρο δεῦρο δεῦρο.

τοροτοροτοροτοροτίξ.   260

κικκαβαῦ κικκαβαῦ.

τοροτοροτοροτορολιλιλίξ.

ΠΙΣΘΕΤΑΙΡΟΣ

ὁρᾷς τιν᾽ ὄρνιν;

ΕΥΕΛΠΙΔΗΣ

μὰ τὸν Ἀπόλλω 'γὼ μὲν οὔ·
καίτοι κέχηνά γ᾽ ἐς τὸν οὐρανὸν βλέπων.

ΠΙΣΘΕΤΑΙΡΟΣ

ἄλλως ἄρ᾽ οὔποψ, ὡς ἔοικ᾽, ἐς τὴν λόχμην   265
ἐσβὰς ἐπῷζε χαραδριὸν μιμούμενος.

ὌΡΝΙΣ ΤΙΣ

τοροτὶξ τοροτίξ.

ΠΙΣΘΕΤΑΙΡΟΣ

ὠγάθ᾽ ἀλλ᾽ εἷς οὑτοσὶ καὶ δή τις ὄρνις ἔρχεται.

ΕΥΕΛΠΙΔΗΣ

νὴ Δί᾽ ὄρνις δῆτα. τίς ποτ᾽ ἐστίν; οὐ δήπου ταῶς;

ΠΙΣΘΕΤΑΙΡΟΣ

οὗτος αὐτὸς νῷν φράσει· τίς ἐστιν ὄρνις οὑτοσί;   270

34

Birds

[The final words gradually change from coherent speech into a bird call]
>Come here, come here,
>come here, come here.
>Toro-toro toro-toro-tix
>Kik-kabau, kik-kabau.   [260]
>Toro-toro toro-toro li-li-lix

[Euelpides and Pisthetairos start looking up into the sky for birds]

PISTHETAIROS
>Seen any birds lately?

EUELPIDES
>   No, by Apollo, I haven't—
>even though I'm staring up into the sky,
>not even blinking.

PISTHETAIROS
>   It seems to me
>that hoopoe bird was just wasting time
>hiding, like a curlew, in that thicket,
>and screaming out his bird calls—
>*[imitating Tereus]* po-poi po-poi

[There is an instant response to Pisthetairos' call from off stage, a loud bird call which really scares Pisthetairos and Euelpides]

BIRD *[offstage]*
>Toro-tix, toro-tix.

PISTHETAIROS
>Hey, my good man, here comes a bird.

[Enter a flamingo, very tall and flaming red-something Pisthetairos and Euelpides have never seen]

EUELPIDES
>   By Zeus,
>that's a bird? What kind would you call that?
>It couldn't be a peacock, could it?

[Tereus re-enters from the thicket]

PISTHETAIROS
>Tereus here will tell us. Hey, my friend,
>what's that bird there?

35

Aristophanes

ΤΗΡΕΥΣ

οὗτος οὐ τῶν ἠθάδων τῶνδ᾽ ὧν ὁρᾶθ᾽ ὑμεῖς ἀεί,
ἀλλὰ λιμναῖος.

ΕΥΕΛΠΙΔΗΣ

βαβαὶ καλός γε καὶ φοινικιοῦς.

ΤΗΡΕΥΣ

εἰκότως γε· καὶ γὰρ ὄνομ᾽ αὐτῷ 'στὶ φοινικόπτερος.

ΕΥΕΛΠΙΔΗΣ

οὗτος ὦ σέ τοι.

ΠΙΣΘΕΤΑΙΡΟΣ

τί βωστρεῖς;

ΕΥΕΛΠΙΔΗΣ

ἕτερος ὄρνις οὑτοσί.

ΠΙΣΘΕΤΑΙΡΟΣ

νὴ Δί᾽ ἕτερος δῆτα χοὗτος ἔξεδρον χρόαν ἔχων.   275
τίς ποτ᾽ ἔσθ᾽ ὁ μουσόμαντις ἄτοπος ὄρνις ὀρειβάτης;

ΤΗΡΕΥΣ

ὄνομα τούτῳ Μῆδός ἐστο.

ΠΙΣΘΕΤΑΙΡΟΣ

Μῆδος; ὦναξ Ἡράκλεις·
εἶτα πῶς ἄνευ καμήλου Μῆδος ὢν εἰσέπτετο;

ΕΥΕΛΠΙΔΗΣ

ἕτερος αὖ λόφον κατειληφώς τις ὄρνις οὑτοσί.

ΠΙΣΘΕΤΑΙΡΟΣ

τί τὸ τέρας τουτί ποτ᾽ ἐστίν; οὐ σὺ μόνος ἄρ᾽ ἦσθ᾽ ἔποψ,
ἀλλὰ χοὗτος ἕτερος;   280

ΤΗΡΕΥΣ

οὑτοσὶ μέν ἐστι Φιλοκλέους
ἐξ ἔποπος, ἐγὼ δὲ τούτου πάππος, ὥσπερ εἰ λέγοις
Ἱππόνικος Καλλίου κἀξ Ἱππονίκου Καλλίας.

36

TEREUS

                      Not your everyday fowl —
the kind you always see. She's a marsh bird.   [270]

EUELPIDES

    My goodness, she's gorgeous — flaming red!

TEREUS

    Naturally, that's why she's called Flamingo.

[A second bird enters, a Peacock]

EUELPIDES *[to Pisthetairos]*
    Hey . . .

PISTHETAIROS

              What is it?

EUELPIDES

                    Another bird's arrived.

PISTHETAIROS

    You're right. By god, this one looks really odd.
    [To Tereus] Who's this bizarre bird-prophet of the Muse,
    this strutter from the hills?

TEREUS

                    He's called the Mede.

PISTHETAIROS

    He's a Mede? By lord Hercules, how come
    a Mede flew here without his camel?

EUELPIDES

    Here's another one . . .

[The next bird enters, another Hoopoe]

                  . . . what a crest of feathers!

PISTHETAIROS *[To Tereus]*
    What's this marvel? You're not the only hoopoe?   [280]
    This here's another one?

TEREUS

                He's my grandson —
son of Philocles the Hoopoe — it's like
those names you pass along, when you call
Hipponicus the son of Callias,
and Callias son of Hipponicus.²¹

ΠΙΣΘΕΤΑΙΡΟΣ
Καλλίας ἄρ' οὗτος οὔρνις ἐστίν· ὡς πτερορρυεῖ.

ΕΥΕΛΠΙΔΗΣ
ἅτε γὰρ ὢν γενναῖος ὑπό τε συκοφαντῶν τίλλεται,   285
αἵ τε θήλειαι προσεκτίλλουσιν αὐτοῦ τὰ πτερά.

ΠΙΣΘΕΤΑΙΡΟΣ
ὦ Πόσειδον ἕτερος αὖ τις βαπτὸς ὄρνις οὑτοσί.
τίς ὀνομάζεταί ποθ' οὗτος;

ΤΗΡΕΥΣ
                                    οὑτοσὶ κατωφαγᾶς.

ΠΙΣΘΕΤΑΙΡΟΣ
ἔστι γὰρ κατωφαγᾶς τις ἄλλος ἢ Κλεώνυμος;

ΕΥΕΛΠΙΔΗΣ
πῶς ἂν οὖν Κλεώνυμός γ' ὢν οὐκ ἀπέβαλε τὸν λόφον;

ΠΙΣΘΕΤΑΙΡΟΣ
ἀλλὰ μέντοι τίς ποθ' ἡ λόφωσις ἡ τῶν ὀρνέων;   291
ἢ 'πὶ τὸν δίαυλον ἦλθον;

ΤΗΡΕΥΣ
                                    ὥσπερ οἱ Κᾶρες μὲν οὖν
ἐπὶ λόφων οἰκοῦσιν ὦγάθ' ἀσφαλείας οὕνεκα.

ΠΙΣΘΕΤΑΙΡΟΣ
ὦ Πόσειδον οὐχ ὁρᾷς ὅσον συνείλεκται κακὸν
ὀρνέων;

ΕΥΕΛΠΙΔΗΣ
                                    ὦναξ Ἄπολλον τοῦ νέφους. ἰοὺ ἰού,   295
οὐδ' ἰδεῖν ἔτ' ἔσθ' ὑπ' αὐτῶν πετομένων τὴν εἴσοδον.

PISTHETAIROS
  So this bird is Callias. His feathers—
  he seems to have lost quite a few.

TEREUS
                    Yes, that's true—
  being a well-off bird he's plucked by parasites,
  and female creatures flock around him, too,
  to yank his plumage out.

[Enter the Glutton-bird, an invented species, very fat and brightly coloured]

PISTHETAIROS
                    By Poseidon,
  here's another bright young bird. What's it called?

TEREUS
  This one's the Glutton-bird.

PISTHETAIROS
                    Another glutton?
  Cleonymus is not the only one?[22]

EUELPIDES
  If this bird were like our Cleonymus,   [290]
  wouldn't he have thrown away his crest?

PISTHETAIROS
  Why do all the birds display such head crests?
  Are they going to run a race in armour?

TEREUS
  No, my dear fellow, they live up on the crests,
  because it's safer, like the Carians.[23]

PISTHETAIROS *[looking offstage]*
  Holy Poseidon, do you see those birds!
  What a fowl bunch of them—all flocking here!

EUELPIDES *[looking in the same direction]*
  Lord Apollo, there's a huge bird cloud! Wow!
  So many feathered wings in there I can't see
  a way through all those feathers to the wings.

*[Enter the Chorus of Birds in a dense mass. Pisthetairos and Euelpides clamber
up the rock to get a better look at them]*

Aristophanes

ΠΙΣΘΕΤΑΙΡΟΣ
οὑτοσὶ πέρδιξ, ἐκεινοσί γε νὴ Δί᾽ ἀτταγᾶς,
οὑτοσὶ δὲ πηνέλοψ, ἐκεινηὶ δέ γ᾽ ἀλκυών.

ΕΥΕΛΠΙΔΗΣ
τίς γάρ ἐσθ᾽ οὕπισθεν αὐτῆς;

ΠΙΣΘΕΤΑΙΡΟΣ
ὅστις ἐστί; κειρύλος.

ΕΥΕΛΠΙΔΗΣ
κειρύλος γάρ ἐστιν ὄρνις;

ΠΙΣΘΕΤΑΙΡΟΣ
οὐ γάρ ἐστι Σποργίλος;   300
χαὐτηί γε γλαῦξ.

ΕΥΕΛΠΙΔΗΣ
τί φής; τίς γλαῦκ᾽ Ἀθήναζ᾽ ἤγαγεν;

ΠΙΣΘΕΤΑΙΡΟΣ
κίττα, τρυγών, κορυδός, ἐλεᾶς,

ΕΥΕΛΠΙΔΗΣ
ὑποθυμὶς, περιστερά,

ΠΙΣΘΕΤΑΙΡΟΣ
νέρτος, ἱέραξ, φάττα,

ΕΥΕΛΠΙΔΗΣ
κόκκυξ, ἐρυθρόπους,

ΠΙΣΘΕΤΑΙΡΟΣ
κεβλήπυρις,

ΕΥΕΛΠΙΔΗΣ
πορφυρὶς, κερχνῄς, κολυμβὶς, ἀμπελὶς, φήην,

ΠΙΣΘΕΤΑΙΡΟΣ
δρύοψ.

40

PISTHETAIROS
               Hey, look at that—
it's a partridge, and that one over there,
by Zeus, a francolin—there's a widgeon—
and that's a halcyon!

EUELPIDES
            What's the one behind her?

PISTHETAIROS
What is it? It's a spotted shaver.

EUELPIDES
                  Shaver?
You mean there's a bird that cuts our hair?

PISTHETAIROS
               Why not?
After all, there's that barber in the city—
the one we all call Sparrow Sporgilos.[24]   [300]
Here comes an owl.

EUELPIDES
        Well, what about that?
Who brings owls to Athens?[25]

PISTHETAIROS *[identifying birds in the crowd]*
            . . . a turtle dove,
a jay, lark, sedge bird . . .

EUELPIDES
           . . . finch, pigeon . . .

PISTHETAIROS
               . . . falcon,
hawk, ring dove . . .

EUELPIDES
          . . . cuckoo, red shank . . .

PISTHETAIROS
               . . . fire-crest . . .

EUELPIDES
. . . porphyrion, kestrel, dabchick, bunting,
vulture, and that one's there's a . . . *[he's stumped]*

PISTHETAIROS
             . . . woodpecker!!

Aristophanes

ΕΥΕΛΠΙΔΗΣ
ἰοὺ ἰοὺ τῶν ὀρνέων, ἰοὺ ἰοὺ τῶν κοψίχων·   305
οἷα πιππίζουσι καὶ τρέχουσι διακεκραγότες.
ἆρ' ἀπειλοῦσίν γε νῷν; οἴμοι, κεχήνασίν γέ τοι
καὶ βλέπουσιν ἐς σὲ κἀμέ.

ΠΙΣΘΕΤΑΙΡΟΣ
                                        τοῦτο μὲν κἀμοὶ δοκεῖ.

ΧΟΡΟΣ
ποποποποποποποποποῖ ποῦ μ' ἄρ' ὃς   310
ἐκάλεσε; τίνα τόπον ἄρα ποτὲ νέμεται;

ΤΗΡΕΥΣ
οὑτοσὶ πάλαι πάρειμι κοὐκ ἀποστατῶ φίλων.

ΧΟΡΟΣ
τί τί τί τί τί τί τί τί· τίνα λόγον ἄρα ποτὲ
πρὸς ἐμὲ φίλον ἔχων;   315

ΤΗΡΕΥΣ
κοινὸν ἀσφαλῆ δίκαιον ἡδὺν ὠφελήσιμον.
ἄνδρε γὰρ λεπτὼ λογιστὰ δεῦρ' ἀφῖχθον ὡς ἐμέ.

ΧΟΡΟΣ
ποῦ; πᾷ; πῶς φῄς;

ΤΗΡΕΥΣ
φήμ' ἀπ' ἀνθρώπων ἀφῖχθαι δεῦρο πρεσβύτα δύο·   320
ἥκετον δ' ἔχοντε πρέμνον πράγματος πελωρίου.

ΧΟΡΟΣ
ὦ μέγιστον ἐξαμαρτὼν ἐξ ὅτου 'τράφην ἐγώ,
πῶς λέγεις;

ΤΗΡΕΥΣ
                        μήπω φοβηθῇς τὸν λόγον.

ΧΟΡΟΣ
                                        τί μ' ἠργάσω;

42

EUELPIDES

What a crowd of birds! A major flock of fowls!
All that twitter as they prance around,
those rival cries! . . . Oh, oh, what's going on?
Are they a threat? They're looking straight at us—
their beaks are open!

PISTHETAIROS

It looks that way to me.

CHORUS LEADER *[starting with a bird call]*

To-toto-to to-toto-to to-to.   [310]
Who's been calling me?
Where's he keep his nest?

TEREUS

I'm the one. I've been waiting here a while.
I've not left my bird friends in the lurch.

CHORUS LEADER

Ti-tit-ti ti-tit-ti ti-ti-ti-ti
tell me as a friend what you have to say.

TEREUS

I have news for all of us—something safe,
judicious, sweet, and profitable.
Two men have just come here to visit me,
two subtle thinkers . . .

CHORUS LEADER *[interrupting]*

What? What are you saying?

TEREUS

I'm telling you two old men have arrived—   [320]
they've come from lands where human beings live
and bring the stalk of a stupendous plan.

CHORUS LEADER

You fool! This is the most disastrous thing
since I was hatched. What are you telling us?

TEREUS

Don't be afraid of what I have to say.

CHORUS LEADER

What have you done to us?

43

ΤΗΡΕΥΣ

ἄνδρ᾽ ἐδεξάμην ἐραστὰ τῆσδε τῆς ξυνουσίας.

ΧΟΡΟΣ

καὶ δέδρακας τοῦτο τοὔργον;   325

ΤΗΡΕΥΣ

καὶ δεδρακώς γ᾽ ἥδομαι.

ΧΟΡΟΣ

κἆστὸν ἤδη που παρ᾽ ἡμῖν;

ΤΗΡΕΥΣ

εἰ παρ᾽ ὑμῖν εἴμ᾽ ἐγώ.

ΧΟΡΟΣ

ἔα ἔα,

προδεδόμεθ᾽ ἀνόσιά τ᾽ ἐπάθομεν·

ὃς γὰρ φίλος ἦν ὁμότροφά θ᾽ ἡμῖν

ἐνέμετο πεδία παρ᾽ ἡμῖν,   330

παρέβη μὲν θεσμοὺς ἀρχαίους,

παρέβη δ᾽ ὅρκους ὀρνίθων·

ἐς δὲ δόλον ἐκάλεσε, παρέβαλέ τ᾽ ἐμὲ παρὰ

γένος ἀνόσιον, ὅπερ ἐξότ᾽ ἐγένετ᾽ ἐπ᾽ ἐμοὶ

πολέμιον ἐτράφη.   335

— ἀλλὰ πρὸς τοῦτον μὲν ἡμῖν ἐστιν ὕστερος λόγος·

τὼ δὲ πρεσβύτα δοκεῖ μοι τώδε δοῦναι τὴν δίκην

διαφορηθῆναί θ᾽ ὑφ᾽ ἡμῶν.

ΠΙΣΘΕΤΑΙΡΟΣ

ὡς ἀπωλόμεσθ᾽ ἄρα.

44

TEREUS
                                  I've welcomed here
two men in love with our society.

CHORUS LEADER
    You dared to do that?

TEREUS
                              Yes, indeed, I did.
And I'm very pleased I did so.

CHORUS LEADER
                    These two men of yours,
    are they among us now?

TEREUS
                              Yes, as surely as I am.

CHORUS [*breaking into a song of indignation*]
          Aiiii, aiiiii
          He's cheated us,
          he's done us wrong.
          That friend of ours,
          who all along
          has fed with us
          in fields we share,   [330]
          now breaks old laws
          and doesn't care.

          We swore a pact
          of all the birds.
          He's now trapped us
          with deceitful words—
          so power goes
          to all our foes,
          that wicked race
          which since its birth
          was raised for war
          with us on earth.

CHORUS LEADER
    We'll have some words with that one later.
    These two old men should get their punishment—
    I think we should give it now. Let's do it—
    rip 'em to pieces, bit by bit.

PISTHETAIROS
                              We're done for.

45

ἘΥΕΛΠΙΔΗΣ

αἴτιος μέντοι σὺ νῷν εἶ τῶν κακῶν τούτων μόνος.

ἐπὶ τί γάρ μ' ἐκεῖθεν ἦγες;

ΠΙΣΘΕΤΑΙΡΟΣ

ἵν' ἀκολουθοίης ἐμοί.   340

ἘΥΕΛΠΙΔΗΣ

ἵνα μὲν οὖν κλάοιμι μεγάλα.

ΠΙΣΘΕΤΑΙΡΟΣ

τοῦτο μὲν ληρεῖς ἔχων

κάρτα· πῶς κλαύσει γάρ, ἢν ἅπαξ γε τώφθαλμὼ 'κκοπῇς;

ΧΟΡΟΣ

ἰὼ ἰώ,

ἔπαγ' ἔπιθ' ἐπίφερε πολέμιον

ὁρμὰν φονίαν, πτέρυγά τε παντᾷ   345

ἐπίβαλε περί τε κύκλωσαι·

ὡς δεῖ τώδ' οἰμώζειν ἄμφω

καὶ δοῦναι ῥύγχει φορβάν.

οὔτε γὰρ ὄρος σκιερὸν οὔτε νέφος αἰθέριον

οὔτε πολιὸν πέλαγος ἔστιν ὅ τι δέξεται   350

τώδ' ἀποφυγόντε με.

— ἀλλὰ μὴ μέλλωμεν ἤδη τώδε τίλλειν καὶ δάκνειν.

ποῦ 'σθ' ὁ ταξίαρχος; ἐπαγέτω τὸ δεξιὸν κέρας.

ἘΥΕΛΠΙΔΗΣ

τοῦτ' ἐκεῖνο· ποῖ φύγω δύστηνος;

ΠΙΣΘΕΤΑΙΡΟΣ

οὗτος οὐ μενεῖς;

ἘΥΕΛΠΙΔΗΣ

ἵν' ὑπὸ τούτων διαφορηθῶ;   355

46

EUELPIDES
>It's all your fault—getting us into this mess.
>Why'd you bring me here?

PISTHETAIROS
>   I wanted you to come.   [340]

EUELPIDES
>What? So I could weep myself to death?

PISTHETAIROS
>Now, you're really talking nonsense—
>how do you intend to weep, once these birds
>poke out your eyes?

CHORUS [*advancing towards Pisthetairos and Euelpides*
>   On, on . . .
>let's move in to attack,
>and launch a bloody rush,
>come in from front and back,
>and break 'em in the crush—
>with wings on every side
>they'll have no place to hide.

>These two will start to howl,
>when my beak starts to eat
>and makes 'em food for fowl.
>There's no well-shaded peak,
>no cloud or salt-grey sea   [350]
>where they can flee from me.

CHORUS LEADER
>Now let's bite and tear these two apart!
>Where's the brigadier? Bring up the right wing!

[*The birds start to close in on Pisthetairos and Euelpides, cowering up on the rocks*]

EUELPIDES
>This is it! I'm done for. Where can I run?

PISTHETAIROS
>Why aren't you staying put?

EUELPIDES
>   Here with you?
>I don't want 'em to rip me into pieces.

47

ΠΙΣΘΕΤΑΙΡΟΣ

　　　　　　　πῶς γὰρ ἂν τούτους δοκεῖς
ἐκφυγεῖν;

ΕΥΕΛΠΙΔΗΣ

　　　οὐκ οἶδ᾽ ὅπως ἄν.

ΠΙΣΘΕΤΑΙΡΟΣ

　　　　　　　　　　ἀλλ᾽ ἐγώ τοί σοι λέγω,
ὅτι μένοντε δεῖ μάχεσθαι λαμβάνειν τε τῶν χυτρῶν.

ΕΥΕΛΠΙΔΗΣ

τί δὲ χύτρα νώ γ᾽ ὠφελήσει;

ΠΙΣΘΕΤΑΙΡΟΣ

　　　　　　　　　　γλαῦξ μὲν οὐ πρόσεισι νῷν.

ΕΥΕΛΠΙΔΗΣ

τοῖς δὲ γαμψώνυξι τοισδί;

ΠΙΣΘΕΤΑΙΡΟΣ

　　　　　　　　　　τὸν ὀβελίσκον ἁρπάσας
εἶτα κατάπηξον πρὸ σαυτοῦ.

ΕΥΕΛΠΙΔΗΣ

　　　　　　　　τοῖσι δ᾽ ὀφθαλμοῖσι τί;　　360

ΠΙΣΘΕΤΑΙΡΟΣ

ὀξύβαφον ἐντευθενὶ προσδοῦ λαβὼν ἢ τρύβλιον.

ΕΥΕΛΠΙΔΗΣ

ὦ σοφώτατ᾽, εὖ γ᾽ ἀνηῦρες αὐτὸ καὶ στρατηγικῶς·
ὑπερακοντίζεις σύ γ᾽ ἤδη Νικίαν ταῖς μηχαναῖς.

ΧΟΡΟΣ

ἐλελελεῦ χώρει κάθες τὸ ῥύγχος· οὐ μέλλειν ἐχρῆν.
ἕλκε τίλλε παῖε δεῖρε, κόπτε πρώτην τὴν χύτραν.　　365

PISTHETAIROS
How do you intend to get away from them?

EUELPIDES
I haven't a clue.

PISTHETAIROS
Then I'll tell you how—
we have to stay right here and fight it out.
So put that cauldron down.

[Pisthetairos takes the cauldron from Euelpides and sets it down on the ground in front of them]

EUELPIDES
What good's a cauldron?

PISTHETAIROS
It'll keep the owls away from us.

EUELPIDES
What about the birds with claws?

PISTHETAIROS *[rummaging in the pack]*
Grab this spit—
stick it in the ground in front of you.

EUELPIDES
How do we protect our eyes?   [360]

PISTHETAIROS *[producing a couple of tin bowls]*
An upturned bowl.
Set this on your head.

EUELPIDES: *[putting the tin bowl upside down on his head and holding up the pot, with the spit stuck in the ground]*
That's brilliant!
What a grand stroke of warlike strategy!
In military matters you're the best—
already smarter than that Nikias.[26]

[Pisthetairos and Euelpides, with tin bowls on their heads, await the birds' charge-with Pisthetairos hiding behind Euelpides, who is holding up the big pot. Their two slaves cower behind them]

CHORUS LEADER
El-el-el-eu . . . Charge!
Keep those beaks level—no holding back now!
Pull 'em, scratch 'em, hit 'em, rip their skins off!
Go smash that big pot first of all.

49

ΤΗΡΕΥΣ

εἰπέ μοι τί μέλλετ᾽ ὦ πάντων κάκιστα θηρίων
ἀπολέσαι παθόντες οὐδὲν ἄνδρε καὶ διασπάσαι
τῆς ἐμῆς γυναικὸς ὄντε ξυγγενεῖ καὶ φυλέτα;

ΧΟΡΟΣ

φεισόμεσθα γάρ τι τῶνδε μᾶλλον ἡμεῖς ἢ λύκων;
ἢ τίνας τεισαίμεθ᾽ ἄλλους τῶνδ᾽ ἂν ἐχθίους ἔτι;   370

ΤΗΡΕΥΣ

εἰ δὲ τὴν φύσιν μὲν ἐχθροὶ τὸν δὲ νοῦν εἰσιν φίλοι,
καὶ διδάξοντές τι δεῦρ᾽ ἥκουσιν ὑμᾶς χρήσιμον;

ΧΟΡΟΣ

πῶς δ᾽ ἂν οἶδ᾽ ἡμᾶς τι χρήσιμον διδάξειάν ποτε
ἢ φράσειαν, ὄντες ἐχθροὶ τοῖσι πάπποις τοῖς ἐμοῖς;

ΤΗΡΕΥΣ

ἀλλ᾽ ἀπ᾽ ἐχθρῶν δῆτα πολλὰ μανθάνουσιν οἱ σοφοί.   375
ἡ γὰρ εὐλάβεια σώζει πάντα. παρὰ μὲν οὖν φίλου
οὐ μάθοις ἂν τοῦθ᾽, ὁ δ᾽ ἐχθρὸς εὐθὺς ἐξηνάγκασεν.
αὐτίχ᾽ αἱ πόλεις παρ᾽ ἀνδρῶν γ᾽ ἔμαθον ἐχθρῶν κοὐ φίλων
ἐκπονεῖν θ᾽ ὑψηλὰ τείχη ναῦς τε κεκτῆσθαι μακράς·
τὸ δὲ μάθημα τοῦτο σώζει παῖδας οἶκον χρήματα.   380

ΧΟΡΟΣ

ἔστι μὲν λόγων ἀκοῦσαι πρῶτον, ὡς ἡμῖν δοκεῖ,
χρήσιμον· μάθοι γὰρ ἄν τις κἀπὸ τῶν ἐχθρῶν σοφόν.

ΠΙΣΘΕΤΑΙΡΟΣ

οἵδε τῆς ὀργῆς χαλᾶν εἴξασιν. ἄναγ᾽ ἐπὶ σκέλος.

*[As the Chorus is about to start its charge, Tereus rushes in between the two
men and the Chorus and tries to stop the Chorus Leader]*

TEREUS

Hold on, you wickedest of animals!
Tell me this: Why do you want to kill these men,
to tear them both to bits? They've done no wrong.
Besides, they're my wife's relatives, her clansmen.

CHORUS LEADER

Why should we be more merciful to them
than we are to wolves? What other animals
are greater enemies of ours than them?
Have we got better targets for revenge?   [370]

TEREUS

Yes, by nature enemies—but what if
they've got good intentions? What if they've come
to teach you something really valuable?

CHORUS LEADER

How could they ever teach us anything,
or tell us something useful—they're enemies,
our feathered forefathers' fierce foes.

TEREUS

But folks with fine minds find from foemen
they can learn a lot. Caution saves us all.
We don't learn that from friends. But enemies
can force that truth upon us right away.
That's why cities learn, not from their allies,
but from enemies, how to build high walls,
assemble fleets of warships—in that way,
their knowledge saves their children, homes, and goods.   [380]

CHORUS LEADER

Well, here's what seems best to me—first of all,
let's hear what they have come to say. It's true—
our enemies can teach us something wise.

PISTHETAIROS *[to Euelpides]*

I think their anger's easing off. Let's retreat.

*[Pisthetairos and Euelpides inch their way toward the doors, still bunched
together, with Euelpides holding up the pot]*

ΤΗΡΕΥΣ
καὶ δίκαιόν γ᾽ ἐστὶ κἀμοὶ δεῖ νέμειν ὑμᾶς χάριν.

ΧΟΡΟΣ
ἀλλὰ μὴν οὐδ᾽ ἄλλο σοί πω πρᾶγμ᾽ ἐνηντιώμεθα.   385

ΠΙΣΘΕΤΑΙΡΟΣ
μᾶλλον εἰρήνην ἄγουσι νὴ Δί᾽, ὥστε τὴν χύτραν
τώ τε τρυβλίω καθίει·
καὶ τὸ δόρυ χρή, τὸν ὀβελίσκον,
περιπατεῖν ἔχοντας ἡμᾶς
τῶν ὅπλων ἐντός, παρ᾽ αὐτὴν   390
τὴν χύτραν ἄκραν ὁρῶντας
ἐγγύς· ὡς οὐ φευκτέον νῷν.

ΕΥΕΛΠΙΔΗΣ
ἐτεὸν ἢν δ᾽ ἄρ᾽ ἀποθάνωμεν,
κατορυχθησόμεσθα ποῦ γῆς;

ΠΙΣΘΕΤΑΙΡΟΣ
ὁ Κεραμεικὸς δέξεται νώ.   395
δημοσίᾳ γὰρ ἵνα ταφῶμεν,
φήσομεν πρὸς τοὺς στρατηγοὺς
μαχομένω τοῖς πολεμίοισιν
ἀποθανεῖν ἐν Ὀρνεαῖς.

ΧΟΡΟΣ
ἄναγ᾽ ἐς τάξιν πάλιν ἐς ταὐτόν,   400
καὶ τὸν θυμὸν κατάθου κύψας
παρὰ τὴν ὀργὴν ὥσπερ ὁπλίτης·
κἀναπυθώμεθα τούσδε τίνες ποτὲ
καὶ πόθεν ἔμολον
ἐπὶ τίνα τ᾽ ἐπίνοιαν.   405
ἰὼ ἔποψ σέ τοι καλῶ.

ΤΗΡΕΥΣ
καλεῖς δὲ τοῦ κλύειν θέλων;

TEREUS *[to the Chorus Leader]*
    It's only fair—and you do owe me a favour,
    out of gratitude.

CHORUS LEADER
                  In other things,
    before today, we've never stood against you.

PISTHETAIROS
    They're acting now more peacefully to us—
    so put that pot and bowl down on the ground.
    But we'd better hang onto the spit, our spear.
    We'll use it on patrol inside our camp   [390]
    right by this cauldron here. Keep your eyes peeled—
    don't even think of flight.

[Euelpides puts down the cauldron, removes his tin-plate helmet, and marches with the spear back and forth by the cauldron, on guard]

EUELPIDES
    What happens if we're killed? Where on earth
    will we be buried?

PISTHETAIROS
                In Kerameikos—
    where the potters live—they'll bury both of us.
    We'll get it done and have the public pay—
    I'll tell the generals we died in battle,
    fighting with the troops at Orneai.[27]

CHORUS LEADER
    Fall back into the ranks you held before.   [400]
    Bend over, and like well-armed soldier boys,
    put your spirit and your anger down.
    We'll look into who these two men may be,
    where they come from, what their intentions are.

[The Chorus of Birds breaks up and retreats]

    Hey, Hoopoe bird, I'm calling you!

TEREUS
               You called?
    What would you like to hear?

ΧΟΡΟΣ

τίνες ποθ' οἵδε καὶ πόθεν;

ΤΗΡΕΥΣ

ξείνω σοφῆς ἀφ' Ἑλλάδος.

ΧΟΡΟΣ

τύχη δὲ ποία κομίζει   410
ποτ' αὐτὼ πρὸς ὄρνιθας
ἐλθεῖν;

ΤΗΡΕΥΣ

     ἔρως
βίου διαίτης τε καὶ
σοῦ ξυνοικεῖν τέ σοι
καὶ ξυνεῖναι τὸ πᾶν.   415

ΧΟΡΟΣ

τί φῄς;
λέγουσι δὴ τίνας λόγους;

ΤΗΡΕΥΣ

ἄπιστα καὶ πέρα κλύειν.

ΧΟΡΟΣ

ὁρᾷ τι κέρδος ἐνθάδ' ἄξιον
μονῆς, ὅτῳ πέποιθ'
ἐμοὶ ξυνὼν
κρατεῖν ἂν ἢ τὸν ἐχθρὸν ἢ   420
φίλοισιν ὠφελεῖν ἔχειν;

ΤΗΡΕΥΣ

λέγει μέγαν τιν' ὄλβον οὔτε
λεκτὸν οὔτε πιστόν· ὡς
σὰ γὰρ τὰ πάντα ταῦτα καὶ
τὸ τῇδε καὶ τὸ κεῖσε καὶ   425
τὸ δεῦρο προσβιβᾷ λέγων.

ΧΟΡΟΣ

πότερα μαινόμενος;

CHORUS LEADER

These two men—
where do they come from and who are they?

TEREUS

These strangers are from Greece, font of wisdom.

CHORUS LEADER

What accident or words   [410]
now brings them to the birds?

TEREUS

The two men love your life,
adore the way you live—
they want to share with you
in all there is to give.

CHORUS LEADER

What's that you just said?
What plan is in their head?

TEREUS

Things you'd never think about—
you'll be amazed—just hear him out.

CHORUS LEADER

He thinks it's good that he
should stay and live with me?
Is he trusting in some plan
to help his fellow man
or thump his enemy?   [420]

TEREUS

He talks of happiness
too great for thought or words
He claims this emptiness—
all space—is for the birds—
here, there, and everywhere.
You'll be convinced, I swear.

CHORUS LEADER

Is he crazy in the head?

ΤΗΡΕΥΣ

ἄφατον ὡς φρόνιμος.

ΧΟΡΟΣ

ἔνι σοφόν τι φρενί;

ΤΗΡΕΥΣ

πυκνότατον κίναδος, 430
σόφισμα κύρμα τρῖμμα παιπάλημ' ὅλον.

ΧΟΡΟΣ

λέγειν λέγειν κέλευέ μοι.
κλύων γὰρ ὧν σύ μοι λέγεις
λόγων ἀνεπτέρωμαι.

ΤΗΡΕΥΣ

ἄγε δὴ σὺ καὶ σὺ τὴν πανοπλίαν μὲν πάλιν 435
ταύτην λαβόντε κρεμάσατον τύχἀγαθῇ
ἐς τὸν ἰπνὸν εἴσω πλησίον τοὐπιστάτου·
σὺ δὲ τούσδ' ἐφ' οἷσπερ τοῖς λόγοις συνέλεξ' ἐγὼ
φράσον, δίδαξον.

ΠΙΣΘΕΤΑΙΡΟΣ

μὰ τὸν Ἀπόλλω 'γὼ μὲν οὔ,
ἢν μὴ διάθωνταί γ' οἵδε διαθήκην ἐμοὶ 440
ἥνπερ ὁ πίθηκος τῇ γυναικὶ διέθετο,
ὁ μαχαιροποιός, μήτε δάκνειν τούτους ἐμὲ
μήτ' ὀρχίπεδ' ἕλκειν μήτ' ὀρύττειν —

ΧΟΡΟΣ

οὔτι που
τόν —; οὐδαμῶς.

ΠΙΣΘΕΤΑΙΡΟΣ

οὔκ, ἀλλὰ τὼφθαλμὼ λέγω.

ΧΟΡΟΣ

διατίθεμαι 'γώ.

ΠΙΣΘΕΤΑΙΡΟΣ

κατόμοσόν νυν ταῦτά μοι.

TEREUS
　He is shrewder than I said.

CHORUS LEADER
　A brilliant thinking box?

TEREUS
　The subtlest, sharpest fox—
　he's been around a lot
　knows every scheme and plot.　　　　　　　　　[430]

CHORUS LEADER
　Ask him to speak to us, to tell us all.
　As I listen now to what you're telling me,
　it makes me feel like flying—taking off!

TEREUS *[to the two slaves]*
　Take their suits of armour in the house—
　hang the stuff up in the kitchen there,
　beside the cooking stool—may it bring good luck!

[turning to Pisthetairos]

　Now you. Lay out your plans—explain to them
　the reason why I called them all together.

[Pisthetairos is struggling with the servants, refusing to give up his armour]

PISTHETAIROS
　No. By Apollo, I won't do it—
　not unless they swear a pact with me
　just like one that monkey Panaitios,　　　　　　[440]
　who makes our knives, had his wife swear to him—
　not to bite or pull my balls or poke me.

CHORUS LEADER
　You mean up your . . .

PISTHETAIROS
　　　　　　No, not there. I mean the eyes.

CHORUS LEADER
　Oh, I'll agree to *that*.

PISTHETAIROS
　　　　　　Then swear an oath on it.

ΧΟΡΟΣ

ὄμνυμ' ἐπὶ τούτοις, πᾶσι νικᾶν τοῖς κριταῖς   445
καὶ τοῖς θεαταῖς πᾶσιν.

ΠΙΣΘΕΤΑΙΡΟΣ

ἔσται ταυταγί.

ΧΟΡΟΣ

εἰ δὲ παραβαίην, ἑνὶ κριτῇ νικᾶν μόνον.
ἀκούετε λεῴ· τοὺς ὁπλίτας νυνμενὶ
ἀνελομένους θὤπλ' ἀπιέναι πάλιν οἴκαδε,
σκοπεῖν δ' ὅ τι ἂν προγράφωμεν ἐν τοῖς πινακίοις.   450

— δολερὸν μὲν ἀεὶ κατὰ πάντα δὴ τρόπον
πέφυκεν ἄνθρωπος· σὺ δ' ὅμως λέγε μοι.
τάχα γὰρ τύχοις ἂν
χρηστὸν ἐξειπὼν ὅ τι μοι παρορᾷς, ἢ
δύναμίν τινα μείζω   455
παραλειπομένην ὑπ' ἐμῆς φρενὸς ἀξυνέτου·
σὺ δὲ τοῦθ' οὐρᾷς λέγ' ἐς κοινόν.
ὃ γὰρ ἂν σὺ τύχῃς μοι
ἀγαθὸν πορίσας, τοῦτο κοινὸν ἔσται.

— ἀλλ' ἐφ' ὅτῳπερ πράγματι τὴν σὴν ἥκεις γνώμην
ἀναπείσας,   460
λέγε θαρρήσας· ὡς τὰς σπονδὰς οὐ μὴ πρότεροι
παραβῶμεν.

ΠΙΣΘΕΤΑΙΡΟΣ

καὶ μὴν ὀργῶ νὴ τὸν Δία καὶ προπεφύραται λόγος εἷς μοι,
ὃν διαμάττειν οὐ κωλύει· φέρε παῖ στέφανον· καταχεῖσθαι
κατὰ χειρὸς ὕδωρ φερέτω ταχύ τις.

ΕΥΕΛΠΙΔΗΣ

δειπνήσειν μέλλομεν; ἢ τί;

CHORUS LEADER
>
> I swear on this condition — that I get
> all the judges' and spectators' votes and win.[28]

PISTHETAIROS
>
> Oh, you'll win!

CHORUS LEADER
>
> And if I break the oath
> then let me win by just a single vote.
> Listen all of you! The armed infantry
> can now pick up their weapons and go home.
> Keep an eye out for any bulletins
> we put up on our notice boards.   [450]

CHORUS *[singing]*
>
> Man's by nature's born to lie.
> But state your case. Give it a try.
> There's a chance you have observed
> some useful things inside this bird,
> some greater power I possess,
> which my dull brain has never guessed.
> So tell all here just what you see.
> If there's a benefit to me,
> we'll share in it communally.

CHORUS LEADER
>
> Tell us the business that's brings you here.   [460]
> Persuade us of your views. So speak right up.
> No need to be afraid — we've made a pact —
> we won't be the ones who break it first.

PISTHETAIROS *[aside to Euelpides]*
>
> By god, I'm full of words, bursting to speak.
> I've worked my speech like well-mixed flour —
> like kneading dough. There's nothing stopping me.
> *[giving instructions to the two slaves]*
> You, lad, fetch me a speaker's wreath — and, you,
> bring water here, so I can wash my hands.

[The two slaves go into the house and return with a wreath and some water]

EUELPIDES *[whispering to Pisthetairos]*
>
> You mean it's time for dinner? What's going on?

ΠΙΣΘΕΤΑΙΡΟΣ

μὰ Δί' ἀλλὰ λέγειν ζητῶ τι πάλαι μέγα καὶ λαρινὸν ἔπος τι,
ὅ το τὴν τούτων θραύσει ψυχήν· οὕτως ὑμῶν ὑπεραλγῶ,
οἵτινες ὄντες πρότερον βασιλῆς — 467

ΧΟΡΟΣ

ἡμεῖς βασιλῆς; τίνος;

ΠΙΣΘΕΤΑΙΡΟΣ

ὑμεῖς
πάντων ὁπόσ' ἔστιν, ἐμοῦ πρῶτον, τουδί, καὶ τοῦ Διὸς
αὐτοῦ,
ἀρχαιότεροι πρότεροί τε Κρόνου καὶ Τιτάνων ἐγένεσθε,
καὶ γῆς.

ΧΟΡΟΣ

καὶ γῆς;

ΠΙΣΘΕΤΑΙΡΟΣ

νὴ τὸν Ἀπόλλω.

ΧΟΡΟΣ

τουτὶ μὰ Δί' οὐκ ἐπεπύσμην.

ΠΙΣΘΕΤΑΙΡΟΣ

ἀμαθὴς γὰρ ἔφυς κοὐ πολυπράγμων, οὐδ' Αἴσωπον
πεπάτηκας, 471
ὃς ἔφασκε λέγων κορυδὸν πάντων πρώτην ὄρνιθα γενέσθαι,
προτέραν τῆς γῆς, κἄπειτα νόσῳ τὸν πατέρ' αὐτῆς
ἀποθνῄσκειν·
γῆν δ' οὐκ εἶναι, τὸν δὲ προκεῖσθαι πεμπταῖον· τὴν δ'
ἀποροῦσαν 474
ὑπ' ἀμηχανίας τὸν πατέρ' αὐτῆς ἐν τῇ κεφαλῇ κατορύξαι.

ΕΥΕΛΠΙΔΗΣ

ὁ πατὴρ ἄρα τῆς κορυδοῦ νυνὶ κεῖται τεθνεὼς Κεφαλῇσιν.

PISTHETAIROS

    For a long time now I've been keen, by god,
    to give them a stupendous speech — overstuffed —
    something to shake their tiny birdy souls.

[Pisthetairos, with the wreath on his head, now turns to the birds and begins his formal oration]

    I'm so sorry for you all, who once were kings . . .

CHORUS LEADER

    Kings? Us? What of?

PISTHETAIROS

           You were kings indeed,
    you ruled over everything there is —
    over him and me, first of all, and then
    over Zeus himself. You see, your ancestry
    goes back before old Kronos and the Titans,
    way back before even Earth herself![29]

CHORUS LEADER

    Before the Earth?

PISTHETAIROS

           Yes, by Apollo.

CHORUS LEADER

    Well, that's something I never knew before!   [470]

PISTHETAIROS

    That's because you're naturally uninformed —
    you lack resourcefulness. You've not read Aesop.
    His story tells us that the lark was born
    before the other birds, before the Earth.
    Her father then grew sick and died. For five days
    he lay there unburied — there was no Earth.
    Not knowing what to do, at last the lark,
    at her wits' end, set him in her own head.

EUELPIDES

    So now, the father of the lark lies dead
    in a headland plot.

ΠΙΣΘΕΤΑΙΡΟΣ

οὔκουν δῆτ᾽ εἰ πρότεροι μὲν γῆς πρότεροι δὲ θεῶν ἐγένοντο,
ὡς πρεσβυτάτων αὐτῶν ὄντων ὀρθῶς ἐσθ᾽ ἡ βασιλεία;

ΕΥΕΛΠΙΔΗΣ

νὴ τὸν Ἀπόλλω· πάνυ τοίνυν χρὴ ῥύγχος βόσκειν σε τὸ
λοιπόν·   479
οὐκ ἀποδώσει ταχέως ὁ Ζεὺς τὸ σκῆπτρον τῷ δρυκολάπτῃ.

ΠΙΣΘΕΤΑΙΡΟΣ

ὡς δ᾽ οὐχὶ θεοὶ τοίνυν ἦρχον τῶν ἀνθρώπων τὸ παλαιόν,
ἀλλ᾽ ὄρνιθες, κἀβασίλευον, πόλλ᾽ ἐστὶ τεκμήρια τούτων.
αὐτίκα δ᾽ ὑμῖν πρῶτ᾽ ἐπιδείξω τὸν ἀλεκτρυόν᾽, ὡς ἐτυράννει
ἦρχέ τε Περσῶν πρῶτον πάντων Δαρείου καὶ Μεγαβάζου,
ὥστε καλεῖται Περσικὸς ὄρνις ἀπὸ τῆς ἀρχῆς ἔτ᾽ ἐκείνης.

ΕΥΕΛΠΙΔΗΣ

διὰ ταῦτ᾽ ἄρ᾽ ἔχων καὶ νῦν ὥσπερ βασιλεὺς ὁ μέγας
διαβάσκει   486
ἐπὶ τῆς κεφαλῆς τὴν κυρβασίαν τῶν ὀρνίθων μόνος ὀρθήν.

ΠΙΣΘΕΤΑΙΡΟΣ

οὕτω δ᾽ ἴσχυσέ τε καὶ μέγας ἦν τότε καὶ πολύς, ὥστ᾽ ἔτι
καὶ νῦν
ὑπὸ τῆς ῥώμης τῆς τότ᾽ ἐκείνης, ὁπόταν μόνον ὄρθριον ᾄσῃ,
ἀναπηδῶσιν πάντες ἐπ᾽ ἔργον χαλκῆς κεραμῆς σκυλοδέψαι
σκυτῆς βαλανῆς ἀλφιταμοιβοὶ τορνευτολυρασπιδοπηγοί·
οἱ δὲ βαδίζουσ᾽ ὑποδησάμενοι νύκτωρ.

ΕΥΕΛΠΙΔΗΣ

                                                    ἐμὲ τοῦτό γ᾽ ἐρώτα.
χλαῖναν γὰρ ἀπώλεσ᾽ ὁ μοχθηρὸς Φρυγίων ἐρίων διὰ
τοῦτον.

PISTHETAIROS

> So if they were born
> before the Earth, before the gods, well then,
> as the eldest, don't they get the right to rule?

EUELPIDES

> By Apollo, yes they do.
> *[addressing the audience]*
> So you out there,
> look ahead and sprout yourselves a beak—
> in good time Zeus will hand his sceptre back   [480]
> to the birds who peck his sacred oaks.

PISTHETAIROS

> Way back then it wasn't gods who ruled.
> They didn't govern men. No. It was the birds.
> There's lots of proof for this. I'll mention here
> example number one—the fighting cock—
> first lord and king of all those Persians,
> well before the time of human kings—
> those Dariuses and Megabazuses.
> Because he was their king, the cock's still called
> the Persian Bird.

EUELPIDES

> That's why to this very day
> the cock's the only bird to strut about
> like some great Persian king, and on his head
> he wears his crown erect.

PISTHETAIROS

> He was so great,
> so mighty and so strong, that even now,
> thanks to his power then, when he sings out
> his early morning song, all men leap up
> to head for work—blacksmiths, potters, tanners,   [490]
> men who deal in corn or supervise the baths,
> or make our shields or fabricate our lyres—
> they all lace on their shoes and set off in the dark.

EUELPIDES

> I can vouch for that! I had some bad luck,
> thanks to that cock—I lost my cloak to thieves,
> a soft and warm one, too, of Phrygian wool.

ἐς δεκάτην γάρ ποτε παιδαρίου κληθεὶς ὑπέπινον ἐν ἄστει,
κἄρτι καθηῦδον, καὶ πρὶν δειπνεῖν τοὺς ἄλλους οὗτος ἄρ᾽
ᾖσεν·   495
κἀγὼ νομίσας ὄρθρον ἐχώρουν Ἀλιμουντάδε, κἄρτι
προκύπτω
ἔξω τείχους καὶ λωποδύτης παίει ῥοπάλῳ με τὸ νῶτον·
κἀγὼ πίπτω μέλλω τε βοᾶν, ὁ δ᾽ ἀπέβλισε θοἰμάτιόν μου.

ΠΙΣΘΕΤΑΙΡΟΣ
ἰκτῖνος δ᾽ οὖν τῶν Ἑλλήνων ἦρχεν τότε κἀβασίλευεν.

ΧΟΡΟΣ
τῶν Ἑλλήνων;   500

ΠΙΣΘΕΤΑΙΡΟΣ
            καὶ κατέδειξέν γ᾽ οὗτος πρῶτος βασιλεύων
προκυλινδεῖσθαι τοῖς ἰκτίνοις.

ΕΥΕΛΠΙΔΗΣ
                            νὴ τὸν Διόνυσον, ἐγὼ γοῦν
ἐκυλινδούμην ἰκτῖνον ἰδών· κᾆθ᾽ ὕπτιος ὢν ἀναχάσκων
ὀβολὸν κατεβρόχθισα· κᾆτα κενὸν τὸν θύλακον οἴκαδ᾽
ἀφεῖλκον.

ΠΙΣΘΕΤΑΙΡΟΣ
Αἰγύπτου δ᾽ αὖ καὶ Φοινίκης πάσης κόκκυξ βασιλεὺς ἦν·
χὠπόθ᾽ ὁ κόκκυξ εἴποι 'κόκκυ,' τότ᾽ ἂν οἱ Φοίνικες
ἅπαντες   505
τοὺς πυροὺς ἂν καὶ τὰς κριθὰς ἐν τοῖς πεδίοις ἐθέριζον.

ΕΥΕΛΠΙΔΗΣ
τοῦτ᾽ ἄρ᾽ ἐκεῖν᾽ ἦν τοὔπος ἀληθῶς· 'κόκκυ ψωλοὶ πεδίονδε.'

ΠΙΣΘΕΤΑΙΡΟΣ
ἦρχον δ᾽ οὕτω σφόδρα τὴν ἀρχήν, ὥστ᾽ εἴ τις καὶ βασιλεύοι
ἐν ταῖς πόλεσιν τῶν Ἑλλήνων Ἀγαμέμνων ἢ Μενέλαος,

I'd been invited to a festive do,
where some child was going to get his name,
right here in the city. I'd had some drinks—
and those drinks, well, they made me fall asleep.
Before the other guests began to eat,
that bird lets rip his cock-a-doodle-doo!
I thought it was the early morning call.
So I run off for Halimus[30]—but then,
just outside the city walls, I get mugged,
some coat thief hits me square across the back—
he used a cudgel! When I fall down there,
about to cry for help, he steals my cloak!

PISTHETAIROS

To resume—way back then the Kite was king.
He ruled the Greeks.

CHORUS LEADER

King of the Greeks!!

PISTHETAIROS

That's right.
As king he was the first to show us how   [500]
to grovel on the ground before a kite.

EUELPIDES

By Dionysus, I once saw a kite
and rolled along the ground, then, on my back,
my mouth wide open, gulped an obol down.
I had to trudge home with an empty sack.[31]

PISTHETAIROS

Take Egypt and Phoenicia—they were ruled
by Cuckoo kings. And when they cried "Cuckoooo!!"
all those Phoenicians harvested their crop—
the wheat and barley in their fields.

EUELPIDES

That's why
if someone's cock is ploughing your wife's field,
we call you "Cuckoo!"—you're being fooled![32]

PISTHETAIROS

The kingship of the birds was then so strong
that in the cities of the Greeks a king—
an Agamemnon, say, or Menelaus—

Aristophanes

ἐπὶ τῶν σκήπτρων ἐκάθητ᾽ ὄρνις μετέχων ὅ τι
δωροδοκοίη.   510

ΕΥΕΛΠΙΔΗΣ
τουτὶ τοίνυν οὐκ ἤδη 'γώ· καὶ δῆτά μ᾽ ἐλάμβανε θαῦμα,
ὁπότ᾽ ἐξέλθοι Πρίαμός τις ἔχων ὄρνιν ἐν τοῖσι τραγῳδοῖς,
ὁ δ᾽ ἄρ᾽ εἱστήκει τὸν Λυσικράτη τηρῶν ὅ τι δωροδοκοίη.

ΠΙΣΘΕΤΑΙΡΟΣ
ὃ δὲ δεινότατόν γ᾽ ἐστὶν ἁπάντων, ὁ Ζεὺς γὰρ ὁ νῦν
βασιλεύων
αἰετὸν ὄρνιν ἕστηκεν ἔχων ἐπὶ τῆς κεφαλῆς βασιλεὺς ὤν,
ἡ δ᾽ αὖ θυγάτηρ γλαῦχ᾽, ὁ δ᾽ Ἀπόλλων ὥσπερ θεράπων
ἱέρακα.   516

ΕΥΕΛΠΙΔΗΣ
νὴ τὴν Δήμητρ᾽ εὖ ταῦτα λέγεις. τίνος οὕνεκα ταῦτ᾽ ἄρ᾽
ἔχουσιν;

ΠΙΣΘΕΤΑΙΡΟΣ
ἵν᾽ ὅταν θύων τις ἔπειτ᾽ αὐτοῖς ἐς τὴν χεῖρ᾽, ὡς νόμος ἐστίν,
τὰ σπλάγχνα διδῷ, τοῦ Διὸς αὐτοὶ πρότεροι τὰ σπλάγχνα
λάβωσιν.
ὤμνυ τ᾽ οὐδεὶς τότ᾽ ἂν ἀνθρώπων θεόν, ἀλλ᾽ ὄρνιθας
ἅπαντες·   520
Λάμπων δ᾽ ὄμνυσ᾽ ἔτι καὶ νυνὶ τὸν χῆν᾽, ὅταν ἐξαπατᾷ τι.
οὕτως ὑμᾶς πάντες πρότερον μεγάλους ἁγίους τ᾽ ἐνόμιζον,
νῦν δ᾽ ἀνδράποδ᾽ ἠλιθίους Μανᾶς·
ὥσπερ δ᾽ ἤδη τοὺς μαινομένους
βάλλουσ᾽ ὑμᾶς, κἀν τοῖς ἱεροῖς   525
πᾶς τις ἐφ᾽ ὑμῖν ὀρνιθευτὴς
ἵστησι βρόχους παγίδας ῥάβδους
ἕρκη νεφέλας δίκτυα πηκτάς·
εἶτα λαβόντες πωλοῦσ᾽ ἀθρόους·
οἱ δ᾽ ὠνοῦνται βλιμάζοντες·   530
κοὐδ᾽ οὖν, εἴπερ ταῦτα δοκεῖ δρᾶν,
ὀπτησάμενοι παρέθενθ᾽ ὑμᾶς,
ἀλλ᾽ ἐπικνῶσιν τυρὸν ἔλαιον
σίλφιον ὄξος καὶ τρίψαντες

66

had a bird perched on his regal sceptre.
And it got its own share of all the gifts   [510]
the king received.

EUELPIDES

        Now, that I didn't know.
I always get amazed in tragedies
when some king Priam comes on with a bird.
I guess it stands on guard there, keeping watch
to see what presents Lysicrates gets.[33]

PISTHETAIROS

Here's the weirdest proof of all—lord Zeus
who now commands the sky, because he's king,
carries an eagle on his head. There's more—
his daughter has an owl, and Apollo,
like a servant, has a hawk.

EUELPIDES

                        That's right,
by Demeter! What's the reason for those birds?

PISTHETAIROS

So when someone makes a sacrifice
and then, in accordance with tradition,
puts the guts into god's hands, the birds
can seize those entrails well before Zeus can.
Back then no man would swear upon the gods—
they swore their oaths on birds. And even now,   [520]
our Lampon seals his promises "By Goose,"
when he intends to cheat.[34] In days gone by,
all men considered you like that—as great
and sacred beings. Now they all think of you
as slaves and fools and useless layabouts.
They throw stones at you, as if you're mad.
And every hunter in the temples there
sets up his traps—all those nooses, gins,
limed sticks and snares, fine mesh and hunting nets,
and cages, too. Then once they've got you trapped,
they sell you by the bunch. Those who come to buy
poke and prod your flesh. If you seem good to eat,   [530]
they don't simply roast you by yourself—no!
They grate on cheese, mix oil and silphium

κατάχυσμ' ἕτερον γλυκὺ καὶ λιπαρόν,   535
κἄπειτα κατεσκέδασαν θερμὸν
τοῦτο καθ' ὑμῶν
αὐτῶν ὥσπερ κενεβρείων.

ΧΟΡΟΣ

πολὺ δὴ πολὺ δὴ χαλεπωτάτους λόγους
ἤνεγκας ἄνθρωφ'· ὡς ἐδάκρυσά γ' ἐμῶν   540
πατέρων κάκην, οἳ
τάσδε τὰς τιμὰς προγόνων παραδόντων
ἐπ' ἐμοῦ κατέλυσαν.
σὺ δέ μοι κατὰ δαίμονα καί τινα συντυχίαν
ἀγαθὴν ἥκεις ἐμοὶ σωτήρ.   545
ἀναθεὶς γὰρ ἐγώ σοι
τὰ νεοττία κἀμαυτὸν οἰκήσω.

— ἀλλ' ὅ τι χρὴ δρᾶν, σὺ δίδασκε παρών· ὡς ζῆν οὐκ ἄξιον
ἡμῖν,
εἰ μὴ κομιούμεθα παντὶ τρόπῳ τὴν ἡμετέραν βασιλείαν.

ΠΙΣΘΕΤΑΙΡΟΣ

καὶ δὴ τοίνυν πρῶτα διδάσκω μίαν ὀρνίθων πόλιν εἶναι,   550
κἄπειτα τὸν ἀέρα πάντα κύκλῳ καὶ πᾶν τουτὶ τὸ μεταξὺ
περιτειχίζειν μεγάλαις πλίνθοις ὀπταῖς ὥσπερ Βαβυλῶνα.

ΕΥΕΛΠΙΔΗΣ

ὦ Κεβριόνη καὶ Πορφυρίων ὡς σμερδαλέον τὸ πόλισμα.

ΠΙΣΘΕΤΑΙΡΟΣ

κἄπειτ' ἢν τοῦτ' ἐπανεστήκῃ, τὴν ἀρχὴν τὸν Δί' ἀπαιτεῖν·
κἂν μὲν μὴ φῇ μηδ' ἐθελήσῃ μηδ' εὐθὺς γνωσιμαχήσῃ,   555
ἱερὸν πόλεμον πρωϋδᾶν αὐτῷ, καὶ τοῖσι θεοῖσιν ἀπειπεῖν

with vinegar—and then whip up a sauce,
oily and sweet, which they pour on you hot,
as if you were a chunk of carrion meat.

CHORUS

This human speaks
of our great pain
our fathers' sins   [540]
we mourn again—
born into rule,
they threw away
what they received,
their fathers' sway.

But now you've come—
fine stroke of fate—
to save our cause.
Here let me state
I'll trust myself
and all my chicks
to help promote
your politics.

CHORUS LEADER

You need to stick around to tell us all
what we should do. Our lives won't be worth living
unless by using every scheme there is
we get back what's ours—our sovereignty.

PISTHETAIROS

Then the first point I'd advise you of is this: [550]
there should be one single city of the birds.
Next, you should encircle the entire air,
all this space between the earth and heaven,
with a huge wall of baked brick—like Babylon.

EUELPIDES

O Kebriones and Porphyrion!
What a mighty place! How well fortified![35]

PISTHETAIROS

When you've completed that, demand from Zeus
he give you back your rule. If he says no,
he doesn't want to and won't sign on at once,
you then declare a holy war on him.

διὰ τῆς χώρας τῆς ὑμετέρας ἐστυκόσι μὴ διαφοιτᾶν,
ὥσπερ πρότερον μοιχεύσοντες τὰς Ἀλκμήνας κατέβαινον
καὶ τὰς Ἀλόπας καὶ τὰς Σεμέλας· ἤνπερ δ' ἐπίωσ',
ἐπιβάλλειν   559
σφραγῖδ' αὐτοῖς ἐπὶ τὴν ψωλήν, ἵνα μὴ βινῶσ' ἔτ' ἐκείνας.
τοῖς δ' ἀνθρώποις ὄρνιν ἕτερον πέμψαι κήρυκα κελεύω,
ὡς ὀρνίθων βασιλευόντων θύειν ὄρνισι τὸ λοιπόν,
κἄπειτα θεοῖς ὕστερον αὖθις· προσνείμασθαι δὲ πρεπόντως
τοῖσι θεοῖσιν τῶν ὀρνίθων ὃς ἂν ἁρμόττῃ καθ' ἕκαστον·
ἢν Ἀφροδίτῃ θύῃ, πυροὺς ὄρνιθι φαληρίδι θύειν·   565
ἢν δὲ Ποσειδῶνί τις οἶν θύῃ, νήττῃ πυροὺς καθαγίζειν·
ἢν δ' Ἡρακλέει θύῃ τι, λάρῳ ναστοὺς θύειν μελιτοῦντας·
κἂν Διὰ θύῃ βασιλεῖ κριόν, βασιλεύς ἐστ' ὀρχίλος ὄρνις,
ᾧ προτέρῳ δεῖ τοῦ Διὸς αὐτοῦ σέρφον ἐνόρχην σφαγιάζειν.

ΕΥΕΛΠΙΔΗΣ
    ἤσθην σέρφῳ σφαγιαζομένῳ. βροντάτω νῦν ὁ μέγας
    Ζάν.   570

ΧΟΡΟΣ
    καὶ πῶς ἡμᾶς νομιοῦσι θεοὺς ἄνθρωποι κοὐχὶ κολοιούς,
    οἳ πετόμεσθα πτέρυγάς τ' ἔχομεν;

ΠΙΣΘΕΤΑΙΡΟΣ
                            ληρεῖς· καὶ νὴ Δί' ὅ γ' Ἑρμῆς
    πέτεται θεὸς ὢν πτέρυγάς τε φορεῖ, κἄλλοι γε θεοὶ πάνυ
    πολλοί.
    αὐτίκα Νίκη πέτεται πτερύγοιν χρυσαῖν καὶ νὴ Δί' Ἔρως
    γε·
    Ἥρην δέ γ' Ὅμηρος ἔφασκ' ἰκέλην εἶναι τρήρωνι
    πελείῃ.   575

Tell those gods they can't come through your space
with cocks erect, the way they used to do,
rushing down to screw another woman —
like Alkmene, Semele, or Alope.[36]
For if you ever catch them coming down
you'll stamp your seal right on their swollen pricks —   [560]
they won't be fucking women any more.
And I'd advise you send another bird
as herald down to human beings to say
that since the birds from now on will be kings,
they have to offer sacrifice to them.
The offerings to the gods take second place.
Then each of the gods must be closely matched
with an appropriate bird. So if a man
is offering Athena holy sacrifice,
he must first give the Coot some barley corn.
If sacrificing sheep to god Poseidon,
let him bring toasted wheat grains to the Duck.
And anyone who's going to sacrifice
to Hercules must give the Cormorant
some honey cakes. A ram for Zeus the king?
Then first, because the Wren is king of birds,
ahead of Zeus himself, his sacrifice
requires the worshipper to execute
an uncastrated gnat.

EUELPIDES
                              I like that bit about
the slaughtered gnat. Now thunder on, great Zan.[37]   [570]

CHORUS LEADER
But how will humans think of us as gods
and not just jackdaws flying around on wings?

PISTHETAIROS
A foolish question. Hermes is a god,
and he has wings and flies — so do others,
all sorts of them. There's Victory, for one,
with wings of gold. And Eros is the same.
Then there's Iris — just like a timorous dove,
that's what Homer says.

71

ΕΥΕΛΠΙΔΗΣ

ὁ Ζεὺς δ' ἡμῖν οὐ βροντήσας πέμψει πτερόεντα κεραυνόν;

ΠΙΣΘΕΤΑΙΡΟΣ

ἢν δ' οὖν ὑμᾶς μὲν ὑπ' ἀγνοίας εἶναι νομίσωσι τὸ μηδέν,
τούτους δὲ θεοὺς τοὺς ἐν Ὀλύμπῳ τότε χρὴ στρούθων
νέφος ἀρθὲν
καὶ σπερμολόγων ἐκ τῶν ἀγρῶν τὸ σπέρμ' αὐτῶν
ἀνακάψαι·
κἄπειτ' αὐτοῖς ἡ Δημήτηρ πυροὺς πεινῶσι μετρείτω.   580

ΕΥΕΛΠΙΔΗΣ

οὐκ ἐθελήσει μὰ Δί', ἀλλ' ὄψει προφάσεις αὐτὴν
παρέχουσαν.

ΠΙΣΘΕΤΑΙΡΟΣ

οἱ δ' αὖ κόρακες τῶν ζευγαρίων, οἷσιν τὴν γῆν καταροῦσιν,
καὶ τῶν προβάτων τοὺς ὀφθαλμοὺς ἐκκοψάντων ἐπὶ πείρᾳ·
εἶθ' ὅ γ' Ἀπόλλων ἰατρός γ' ὢν ἰάσθω· μισθοφορεῖ δέ.

ΕΥΕΛΠΙΔΗΣ

μὴ πρίν γ' ἂν ἐγὼ τὼ βοιδαρίω τὠμὼ πρώτιστ'
ἀποδῶμαι.   585

ΠΙΣΘΕΤΑΙΡΟΣ

ἢν δ' ἡγῶνται σὲ θεὸν σὲ βίον σὲ δὲ γῆν σὲ Κρόνον σὲ
Ποσειδῶ,
ἀγάθ' αὐτοῖσιν πάντα παρέσται.

ΧΟΡΟΣ

λέγε δή μοι τῶν ἀγαθῶν ἕν.

ΠΙΣΘΕΤΑΙΡΟΣ

πρῶτα μὲν αὐτῶν τὰς οἰνάνθας οἱ πάρνοπες οὐ κατέδονται,
ἀλλὰ γλαυκῶν λόχος εἰς αὐτοὺς καὶ κερχνῄδων ἐπιτρίψει.
εἶθ' οἱ κνῖπες καὶ ψῆνες ἀεὶ τὰς συκᾶς οὐ κατέδονται,   590
ἀλλ' ἀναλέξει πάντας καθαρῶς αὐτοὺς ἀγέλη μία κιχλῶν.

EUELPIDES

                    But what if Zeus
lets his thunder peal, then fires down on us
his lightning bolt—that's got wings as well.

PISTHETAIROS *[ignoring Euelpides]*
    Now, if men in their stupidity
think nothing of you and keep worshipping
Olympian gods, then a large cloud of birds,
of rooks and sparrows, must attack their farms,
devouring all the seed. And as they starve,
let Demeter then dole out grain to them.   [580]

EUELPIDES
    She won't be willing to do that, by Zeus.
She'll make excuses—as you'll see.

PISTHETAIROS
                      Then as a test,
the ravens can peck out their livestock's eyes,
the ones that pull the ploughs to work the land,
and other creatures, too. Let Apollo
make them better—he's the god of healing.
That's why he gets paid.

EUELPIDES
                But you can't do this
'til I've sold my two little oxen first.

PISTHETAIROS
    But if they think of you as god, as life,
as Earth, as Kronos and Poseidon, too,
then all good things will come to them.

CHORUS LEADER
                Tell me
what these good things are.

PISTHETAIROS
                 Well, for starters,
locusts won't eat the blossoms on their vines.
The owls and kestrels in just one platoon
will rid them of those pests. Mites and gall wasps   [590]
won't devour the figs. One troop of thrushes
will eradicate them one and all.

ΧΟΡΟΣ
Aristophanes

ΧΟΡΟΣ

πλουτεῖν δὲ πόθεν δώσομεν αὐτοῖς; καὶ γὰρ τούτου σφόδρ'
ἐρῶσιν.

ΠΙΣΘΕΤΑΙΡΟΣ

τὰ μέταλλ' αὐτοῖς μαντευομένοις οὗτοι δώσουσι τὰ χρηστά,
τάς τ' ἐμπορίας τὰς κερδαλέας πρὸς τὸν μάντιν κατεροῦσιν,
ὥστ' ἀπολεῖται τῶν ναυκλήρων οὐδείς.   595

ΧΟΡΟΣ
                               πῶς οὐκ ἀπολεῖται;

ΠΙΣΘΕΤΑΙΡΟΣ

προερεῖ τις ἀεὶ τῶν ὀρνίθων μαντευομένῳ περὶ τοῦ πλοῦ·
'νυνὶ μὴ πλεῖ, χειμὼν ἔσται·' 'νυνὶ πλεῖ, κέρδος ἐπέσται.'

ΕΥΕΛΠΙΔΗΣ

γαῦλον κτῶμαι καὶ ναυκληρῶ, κοὐκ ἂν μείναιμι παρ' ὑμῖν.

ΠΙΣΘΕΤΑΙΡΟΣ

τοὺς θησαυρούς τ' αὐτοῖς δείξουσ' οὓς οἱ πρότεροι κατέθεντο
τῶν ἀργυρίων· οὗτοι γὰρ ἴσασι· λέγουσι δέ τοι τάδε
     πάντες,   600
'οὐδεὶς οἶδεν τὸν θησαυρὸν τὸν ἐμὸν πλὴν εἴ τις ἄρ' ὄρνις.'

ΕΥΕΛΠΙΔΗΣ

πωλῶ γαῦλον, κτῶμαι σμινύην, καὶ τὰς ὑδρίας ἀνορύττω.

ΧΟΡΟΣ

πῶς δ' ὑγιείαν δώσουσ' αὐτοῖς, οὖσαν παρὰ τοῖσι θεοῖσιν;

ΠΙΣΘΕΤΑΙΡΟΣ

ἢν εὖ πράττωσ', οὐχ ὑγιεία μεγάλη τοῦτ' ἐστί;

ΕΥΕΛΠΙΔΗΣ
                                          σάφ' ἴσθι,
ὡς ἄνθρωπός γε κακῶς πράττων ἀτεχνῶς οὐδεὶς
     ὑγιαίνει.   605

74

CHORUS LEADER
But how will we make people wealthy?
That's what they mostly want.

PISTHETAIROS
When people come
petitioning your shrines, the birds can show
the mining sites that pay. They'll tell the priest
the profitable routes for trade. That way
no captain of a ship will be wiped out.

CHORUS LEADER
Why won't those captains come to grief?

PISTHETAIROS
They'll always ask the birds about the trip.
Their seer will say, "A storm is on the way.
Don't sail just yet" or "Now's the time to sail—
you'll turn a tidy profit."

EUELPIDES
Hey, that's for me—
I'll buy a merchant ship and take command.
I won't be staying with you.

PISTHETAIROS
Birds can show men
the silver treasures of their ancestors,
buried in the ground so long ago.
For birds know where these are. Men always say,   [600]
"No one knows where my treasure lies, no one,
except perhaps some bird."

EUELPIDES
I'll sell my boat.
I'll buy a spade and dig up tons of gold.

CHORUS LEADER
How will we provide for human health?
Such things dwell with the gods.

PISTHETAIROS
If they're doing well,
is that not giving them good health?

EUELPIDES
You're right.
A man whose business isn't very sound
is never medically well.

ΧΟΡΟΣ

πῶς δ' ἐς γῆράς ποτ' ἀφίξονται; καὶ γὰρ τοῦτ' ἔστ' ἐν
Ὀλύμπῳ·
ἢ παιδάρι' ὄντ' ἀποθνήσκειν δεῖ;

ΠΙΣΘΕΤΑΙΡΟΣ

μὰ Δί' ἀλλὰ τριακόσι' αὐτοῖς
ἔτι προσθήσουσ' ὄρνιθες ἔτη.

ΤΗΡΕΥΣ

παρὰ τοῦ;

ΠΙΣΘΕΤΑΙΡΟΣ

παρ' ὅτου; παρ' ἑαυτῶν.
οὐκ οἶσθ' ὅτι πέντ' ἀνδρῶν γενεὰς ζώει λακέρυζα κορώνη;

ΕΥΕΛΠΙΔΗΣ

αἰβοῖ πολλῷ κρείττους οὗτοι τοῦ Διὸς ἡμῖν βασιλεύειν.

ΠΙΣΘΕΤΑΙΡΟΣ

οὐ γὰρ πολλῷ;   611
πρῶτον μέν γ' οὐχὶ νεὼς ἡμᾶς
οἰκοδομεῖν δεῖ λιθίνους αὐτοῖς,
οὐδὲ θυρῶσαι χρυσαῖσι θύραις,
ἀλλ' ὑπὸ θάμνοις καὶ πρινιδίοις   615
οἰκήσουσιν. τοῖς δ' αὖ σεμνοῖς
τῶν ὀρνίθων δένδρον ἐλάας
ὁ νεὼς ἔσται· κοὐκ ἐς Δελφοὺς
οὐδ' εἰς Ἄμμων' ἐλθόντες ἐκεῖ
θύσομεν, ἀλλ' ἐν ταῖσιν κομάροις   620
καὶ τοῖς κοτίνοις στάντες ἔχοντες
κριθὰς πυροὺς εὐξόμεθ' αὐτοῖς
ἀνατείνοντες τὼ χεῖρ' ἀγαθῶν
διδόναι τι μέρος· καὶ ταῦθ' ἡμῖν
παραχρῆμ' ἔσται   625
πυροὺς ὀλίγους προβαλοῦσιν.

ΧΟΡΟΣ

ὦ φίλτατ' ἐμοὶ πολὺ πρεσβυτῶν ἐξ ἐχθίστου μεταπίπτων,
οὐκ ἔστιν ὅπως ἂν ἐγώ ποθ' ἑκὼν τῆς σῆς γνώμης ἔτ'
ἀφείμην.

76

CHORUS LEADER

All right,
but how will they get old? That's something, too,
Olympian gods bestow. Must they die young?

PISTHETAIROS

No, no, by god. The birds will add on years,
three hundred more.

CHORUS LEADER

And where will those come from?

PISTHETAIROS

From the birds' supply. You know the saying,
"Five human lifetimes lives the cawing crow."[38]

EUELPIDES

My word, these birds are much more qualified   [610]
to govern us than Zeus.

PISTHETAIROS

Far better qualified!
First, we don't have to build them holy shrines,
made out of stone, or put up golden doors
to decorate their sanctuaries. They live
beneath the bushes and young growing trees.
As for the prouder birds, an olive grove
will be their temple. When we sacrifice,
no need to go to Ammon or to Delphi—
we'll just stand among arbutus trees   [620]
or oleasters with an offering—
barley grains or wheat—uttering our prayers,
our arms outstretched, so from them we receive
our share of benefits. And these we'll gain
by throwing them a few handfuls of grain.

CHORUS LEADER

Old man, how much you've been transformed for me—
From my worst enemy into my friend,
my dearest friend. These strategies of yours—
I'll not abandon them, not willingly.

— ἐπαυχήσας δὲ τοῖσι σοῖς λόγοις
ἐπηπείλησα καὶ κατώμοσα, 630
ἢν σὺ παρ' ἐμὲ θέμενος
ὁμόφρονας λόγους δικαίους
ἀδόλους ὁσίους
ἐπὶ θεοὺς ἴῃς, ἐμοὶ
φρονῶν ξυνῳδά, μὴ πολὺν χρόνον 635
θεοὺς ἔτι σκῆπτρα τἀμὰ τρύψειν.

— ἀλλ' ὅσα μὲν δεῖ ῥώμῃ πράττειν, ἐπὶ ταῦτα τεταξόμεθ' ἡμεῖς·
ὅσα δὲ γνώμῃ δεῖ βουλεύειν, ἐπὶ σοὶ τάδε πάντ' ἀνάκειται.

ΠΙΣΘΕΤΑΙΡΟΣ

καὶ μὴν μὰ τὸν Δί' οὐχὶ νυστάζειν ἔτι
ὥρα 'στὶν ἡμῖν οὐδὲ μελλονικιᾶν, 640
ἀλλ' ὡς τάχιστα δεῖ τι δρᾶν·

ΤΗΡΕΥΣ

                        πρῶτον δέ γε
εἰσέλθετ' ἐς νεοττιάν γε τὴν ἐμὴν
καὶ τἀμὰ κάρφη καὶ τὰ παρόντα φρύγανα,
καὶ τοὔνομ' ἡμῖν φράσατον.

ΠΙΣΘΕΤΑΙΡΟΣ

                        ἀλλὰ ῥᾴδιον.
ἐμοὶ μὲν ὄνομα Πισθέταιρος.

ΤΗΡΕΥΣ

                        τῳδεδὶ;

ΕΥΕΛΠΙΔΗΣ

Εὐελπίδης Κριῶθεν.

ΤΗΡΕΥΣ

                        ἀλλὰ χαίρετον 645
ἄμφω.

ΠΙΣΘΕΤΑΙΡΟΣ καὶ ΕΥΕΛΠΙΔΗΣ
            δεχόμεθα.

ΤΗΡΕΥΣ

            δεῦρο τοίνυν εἴσιτον.

78

CHORUS
>The words you've said make us rejoice—
>and so we'll swear with just one voice
>an oath that if you stand with me—   [630]
>our thoughts and aims in unity—
>honest, pious, just, sincere,
>to go against the gods up there,
>if we're both singing the same song
>the gods won't have my sceptre long.

CHORUS LEADER
>Whatever can be done with force alone
>we're ready to take on—what requires brains
>or thinking through, all that stuff's up to you.

PISTHETAIROS
>That's right, by Zeus. No time for dozing now,   [640]
>or entertaining doubts, like Nikias.[39]
>No—let's get up and at it fast.

TEREUS
>But first, you must come in this nest of mine,
>these sticks and twigs assembled here. So now,
>both of you, tell us your names.

PISTHETAIROS
>   That's easy.
>My name's Pisthetairos.

TEREUS
>   And this man here?

EUELPIDES
>I'm Euelpides, from Crioa.

TEREUS
>Welcome both of you!

PISTHETAIROS and EUELPIDES
>   Thanks very much.

TEREUS
>Won't you come in?

ΠΙΣΘΕΤΑΙΡΟΣ

ἴωμεν· εἰσηγοῦ σὺ λαβὼν ἡμᾶς.

ΤΗΡΕΥΣ

ἴθι.

ΠΙΣΘΕΤΑΙΡΟΣ

ἀτὰρ τὸ δεῖνα, δεῦρ᾽ ἐπανάκρουσαι πάλιν.
φέρ᾽ ἴδω, φράσον νῷν, πῶς ἐγώ τε χοὐτοσὶ
ξυνεσόμεθ᾽ ὑμῖν πετομένοις οὐ πετομένω;   650

ΤΗΡΕΥΣ

καλῶς.

ΠΙΣΘΕΤΑΙΡΟΣ

ὅρα νυν, ὡς ἐν Αἰσώπου λόγοις
ἐστὶν λεγόμενον δή τι, τὴν ἀλώπεχ᾽, ὡς
φλαύρως ἐκοινώνησεν αἰετῷ ποτέ.

ΤΗΡΕΥΣ

μηδὲν φοβηθῇς· ἔστι γάρ τι ῥιζίον,
ὃ διατραγόντ᾽ ἔσεσθον ἐπτερωμένω.   655

ΠΙΣΘΕΤΑΙΡΟΣ

οὕτω μὲν εἰσίωμεν. ἄγε δὴ Ξανθία
καὶ Μανόδωρε λαμβάνετε τὰ στρώματα.

ΧΟΡΟΣ

οὗτος σὲ καλῶ, σὲ λέγω.

ΤΗΡΕΥΣ

τί καλεῖς;

ΧΟΡΟΣ

τούτους μὲν ἄγων μετὰ σαυτοῦ
ἀρίστισον εὖ· τὴν δ᾽ ἡδυμελῆ ξύμφωνον ἀηδόνα Μούσαις
κατάλειφ᾽ ἡμῖν δεῦρ᾽ ἐκβιβάσας, ἵνα παίσωμεν μετ᾽ ἐκείνης.

PISTHETAIROS

               Let's go. But you go first—
show us the way.

TEREUS

           Come on, then.

[Tereus enters his house]

PISTHETAIROS *[holding back, calling into the house]*

                        But . . . it's strange . . .
Come back a minute.

[Tereus reappears at the door]

                 Look, tell us both
how me and him can share the place with you
when you can fly but we're not able to.   [650]

TEREUS

    I don't see any problem there.

PISTHETAIROS

                   Maybe,
but in Aesop's fables there's a story told
about some fox who hung around an eagle,
with unfortunate results.

TEREUS

              Don't be afraid.
We have a little root you nibble on—
and then you'll grow some wings.

PISTHETAIROS

                 All right then,
let's go. *[To the slaves]* Manodorus, Xanthias,
bring in our mattresses.

CHORUS LEADER *[to Tereus]*

              Hold on a second—
I'm calling you.

TEREUS

           Why are you calling me?

CHORUS LEADER

    Take those two men in—give 'em a good meal.
But bring your tuneful nightingale out here,
who with the Muses sings such charming songs—
leave her with us so we can play together.   [660]

ΠΙΣΘΕΤΑΙΡΟΣ
ὦ τοῦτο μέντοι νὴ Δί᾽ αὐτοῖσιν πιθοῦ· 661
ἐκβίβασον ἐκ τοῦ βουτόμου τοὐρνίθιον.

ΕΥΕΛΠΙΔΗΣ
ἐκβίβασον αὐτοῦ πρὸς θεῶν αὐτήν, ἵνα
καὶ νὼ θεασώμεσθα τὴν ἀηδόνα.

ΤΗΡΕΥΣ
ἀλλ᾽ εἰ δοκεῖ σφῷν, ταῦτα χρὴ δρᾶν. ἡ Πρόκνη 665
ἔκβαινε καὶ σαυτὴν ἐπιδείκνυ τοῖς ξένοις.

ΠΙΣΘΕΤΑΙΡΟΣ
ὦ Ζεῦ πολυτίμηθ᾽ ὡς καλὸν τοὐρνίθιον,
ὡς δ᾽ ἁπαλόν, ὡς δὲ λευκόν.

ΕΥΕΛΠΙΔΗΣ
ἆρά γ᾽ οἶσθ᾽ ὅτι
ἐγὼ διαμηρίζοιμ᾽ ἂν αὐτὴν ἡδέως;

ΠΙΣΘΕΤΑΙΡΟΣ
ὅσον δ᾽ ἔχει τὸν χρυσόν, ὥσπερ παρθένος. 670

ΕΥΕΛΠΙΔΗΣ
ἐγὼ μὲν αὐτὴν κἂν φιλῆσαί μοι δοκῶ.

ΠΙΣΘΕΤΑΙΡΟΣ
ἀλλ᾽ ὦ κακόδαιμον ῥύγχος ὀβελίσκοιν ἔχει.

ΕΥΕΛΠΙΔΗΣ
ἀλλ᾽ ὥσπερ ᾠὸν νὴ Δί᾽ ἀπολέψαντα χρὴ
ἀπὸ τῆς κεφαλῆς τὸ λέμμα κᾆθ᾽ οὕτω φιλεῖν.

ΤΗΡΕΥΣ
ἴωμεν. 675

ΠΙΣΘΕΤΑΙΡΟΣ
ἡγοῦ δὴ σὺ νῷν τύχἀγαθῇ.

PISTHETAIROS
> Yes, by god—agree to their request.
> Bring out your little birdie in the reeds.

EUELPIDES
> For gods' sake, bring her out, so we can see
> this lovely nightingale of yours.

TEREUS
> If that's what you both want, it must be done.
> *[calling inside]*
> Come here, Procne. Our guests are calling you.

[Enter Procne from the house. She has a nightingale's head and wings but the body of a young woman. She is wearing gold jewellery]

PISTHETAIROS
> Holy Zeus, that's one gorgeous little bird!
> What a tender chick!

EUELPIDES
> How I'd love to help that birdie
> spread her legs, if you catch my drift.

PISTHETAIROS
> Look at that—
> all the gold she's wearing—just like a girl.   [670]

EUELPIDES
> What I'd like to do right now is kiss her.

PISTHETAIROS
> You idiot—look at that beak she's got,
> a pair of skewers.

EUELPIDES
> All right, by god,
> we'll treat her like an egg—peel off the shell,
> take it clean off her head, and then we'll kiss her.

TEREUS
> Let's get inside.

PISTHETAIROS
> You lead us in—good luck to all!

[Pisthetairos, Euelpides, Tereus, Xanthias, and Manodorus enter the house]

ΧΟΡΟΣ

ὦ φίλη, ὦ ξουθή,
ὦ φίλτατον ὀρνέων
πάντων, ξύννομε τῶν ἐμῶν
ὕμνων, ξύντροφ᾽ ἀηδοῖ,
ἦλθες ἦλθες ὤφθης,   680
ἡδὺν φθόγγον ἐμοὶ φέρουσ᾽.
ἀλλ᾽ ὦ καλλιβόαν κρέκουσ᾽
αὐλὸν φθέγμασιν ἠρινοῖς,
ἄρχου τῶν ἀναπαίστων.

— ἄγε δὴ φύσιν ἄνδρες ἀμαυρόβιοι, φύλλων γενεᾷ
προσόμοιοι,   685
ὀλιγοδρανέες, πλάσματα πηλοῦ, σκιοειδέα φῦλ᾽ ἀμενηνά,
ἀπτῆνες ἐφημέριοι ταλαοὶ βροτοὶ ἀνέρες εἰκελόνειροι,
προσέχετε τὸν νοῦν τοῖς ἀθανάτοις ἡμῖν τοῖς αἰὲν ἐοῦσιν,
τοῖς αἰθερίοις τοῖσιν ἀγήρῳς τοῖς ἄφθιτα μηδομένοισιν,
ἵν᾽ ἀκούσαντες πάντα παρ᾽ ἡμῶν ὀρθῶς περὶ τῶν
μετεώρων.   690
φύσιν οἰωνῶν γένεσίν τε θεῶν ποταμῶν τ᾽ Ἐρέβους τε
Χάους τε
εἰδότες ὀρθῶς, Προδίκῳ παρ᾽ ἐμοῦ κλάειν εἴπητε τὸ λοιπόν.
Χάος ἦν καὶ Νὺξ Ἔρεβός τε μέλαν πρῶτον καὶ Τάρταρος
εὐρύς,
γῆ δ᾽ οὐδ᾽ ἀὴρ οὐδ᾽ οὐρανὸς ἦν· Ἐρέβους δ᾽ ἐν ἀπείροσι
κόλποις
τίκτει πρώτιστον ὑπηνέμιον Νὺξ ἡ μελανόπτερος
ᾠόν,   695
ἐξ οὗ περιτελλομέναις ὥραις ἔβλαστεν Ἔρως ὁ ποθεινός,
στίλβων νῶτον πτερύγοιν χρυσαῖν, εἰκὼς ἀνεμώκεσι δίναις.
οὗτος δὲ Χάει πτερόεντι μιγεὶς νυχίῳ κατὰ Τάρταρον εὐρὺν
ἐνεόττευσεν γένος ἡμέτερον, καὶ πρῶτον ἀνήγαγεν ἐς φῶς.
πρότερον δ᾽ οὐκ ἦν γένος ἀθανάτων, πρὶν Ἔρως ξυνέμειξεν
ἅπαντα·   700

CHORUS [*singing to Procne*]
    Ah, my tawny throated love,
    of all the birds that fly above
    you're dearest to my heart
    your sweet melodious voice
    in my song plays its part—
    my lovely Nightingale,
        you've come,   [680]
        you've come.
    And now you're here with me.
    Pour forth your melody.
    Pipe out the lovely sounds of spring,
    a prelude to my rhythmic speech
    in every melody you sing.

[*Procne plays on the flute for a few moments as the Chorus Leader prepares to address the audience directly. He steps forward getting close to the spectators*]

CHORUS LEADER
    Come now, you men out there, who live such dark, sad lives—
    you're frail, just like a race of leaves—you're shaped from clay,
    you tribes of insubstantial shadows without wings,
    you creatures of a day, unhappy mortal men,
    you figures from a dream, now turn your minds to us,
    the eternal, deathless, air-borne, ageless birds,
    whose wisdom never dies, so you may hear from us
    the truth about celestial things, about the birds—   [690]
    how they sprang into being, how the gods arose,
    how rivers, Chaos, and dark Erebus were formed[40]—
    about all this you'll learn the truth. And so from me
    tell Prodicus in future to depart.[41] At the start,
    there was Chaos, and Night, and pitch-black Erebus,
    and spacious Tartarus. There was no earth, no heaven,
    no atmosphere. Then in the wide womb of Erebus,
    that boundless space, black-winged Night, first creature born,
    made pregnant by the wind, once laid an egg. It hatched,
    when seasons came around, and out of it sprang Love—
    the source of all desire, on his back the glitter
    of his golden wings, just like the swirling whirlwind.
    In broad Tartarus, Love had sex with murky Chaos.
    From them our race was born—our first glimpse of the light.
    Before that there was no immortal race at all,
    not before Love mixed all things up. But once they'd bred   [700]

ξυμμιγνυμένων δ' ἑτέρων ἑτέροις γένετ' οὐρανὸς ὠκεανός τε
καὶ γῆ πάντων τε θεῶν μακάρων γένος ἄφθιτον. ὧδε μέν
ἐσμεν
πολὺ πρεσβύτατοι πάντων μακάρων. ἡμεῖς δ' ὡς ἐσμὲν
Ἔρωτος
πολλοῖς δῆλον· πετόμεσθά τε γὰρ καὶ τοῖσιν ἐρῶσι
σύνεσμεν·
πολλοὺς δὲ καλοὺς ἀπομωμοκότας παῖδας πρὸς τέρμασιν
ὥρας   705
διὰ τὴν ἰσχὺν τὴν ἡμετέραν διεμήρισαν ἄνδρες ἐρασταί,
ὁ μὲν ὄρτυγα δοὺς ὁ δὲ πορφυρίων' ὁ δὲ χῆν' ὁ δὲ Περσικὸν
ὄρνιν.
πάντα δὲ θνητοῖς ἐστιν ἀφ' ἡμῶν τῶν ὀρνίθων τὰ μέγιστα.
πρῶτα μὲν ὥρας φαίνομεν ἡμεῖς ἦρος χειμῶνος ὀπώρας·
σπείρειν μέν, ὅταν γέρανος κρώζουσ' ἐς τὴν Λιβύην
μεταχωρῇ.   710
καὶ πηδάλιον τότε ναυκλήρῳ φράζει κρεμάσαντι καθεύδειν,
εἶτα δ' Ὀρέστῃ χλαῖναν ὑφαίνειν, ἵνα μὴ ῥιγῶν ἀποδύῃ.
ἰκτῖνος δ' αὖ μετὰ ταῦτα φανεὶς ἑτέραν ὥραν ἀποφαίνει,
ἡνίκα πεκτεῖν ὥρα προβάτων πόκον ἠρινόν· εἶτα χελιδών,
ὅτε χρὴ χλαῖναν πωλεῖν ἤδη καὶ ληδάριόν τι πρίασθαι. 715
ἐσμὲν δ' ὑμῖν Ἄμμων Δελφοὶ Δωδώνη Φοῖβος Ἀπόλλων.
ἐλθόντες γὰρ πρῶτον ἐπ' ὄρνις οὕτω πρὸς ἅπαντα τρέπεσθε,
πρός τ' ἐμπορίαν, καὶ πρὸς βιότου κτῆσιν, καὶ πρὸς γάμον
ἀνδρός.
ὄρνιν τε νομίζετε πάνθ' ὅσαπερ περὶ μαντείας διακρίνει·
φήμη γ' ὑμῖν ὄρνις ἐστί, πταρμόν τ' ὄρνιθα καλεῖτε,   720
ξύμβολον ὄρνιν, φωνὴν ὄρνιν, θεράποντ' ὄρνιν, ὄνον ὄρνιν.
ἆρ' οὐ φανερῶς ἡμεῖς ὑμῖν ἐσμὲν μαντεῖος Ἀπόλλων;

— ἢν οὖν ἡμᾶς νομίσητε θεούς,
ἕξετε χρῆσθαι μάντεσι Μούσαις
αὔραις ὥραις χειμῶνι θέρει   725
μετρίῳ πνίγει· κοὐκ ἀποδράντες
καθεδούμεθ' ἄνω σεμνυνόμενοι
παρὰ ταῖς νεφέλαις ὥσπερ χὠ Ζεύς·

and blended in with one another, Heaven was born,
Ocean and Earth—and all that clan of deathless gods.
Thus, we're by far the oldest of all blessed ones,
for we are born from Love. There's lots of proof for this.
We fly around the place, assisting those in love—
the handsome lads who swear they'll never bend for sex,
but who, as their young charms come to an end, agree
to let male lovers bugger them, thanks to the birds,
our power as gifts—one man gives a porphyrion,
another man a quail, a third one gives a goose,
and yet another offers up a Persian Fowl.⁴²
All mortals' greatest benefits come from us birds.
The first is this: we make the season known—springtime,
winter, autumn—it's time to sow, as soon as Crane
migrates to Lybia with all that noise. He tells   [710]
the master mariner to hang his rudder up
and go to sleep awhile. He tells Orestes, too,
to weave himself a winter cloak, so he won't freeze
when he sets out again to rip off people's clothes.⁴³
Then after that the Kite appears, to let you know
another season's here—it's time to shear the sheep.
Then Swallow comes. Now you should sell your winter cloak
and get yourself a light one. So we're your Ammon,
Delphi and Dodona—we're your Apollo, too.⁴⁴
See how, in all your business, you first look to birds—
when you trade, buy goods, or when a man gets married.
Whatever you think matters in a prophecy,
you label that a bird—to you, Rumour's a bird;   [720]
you say a sneeze or a chance meeting is a bird,
a sound's a bird, a servant's a bird—and so's an ass.
It's clear you look on us as your Apollo.

CHORUS

So you ought to make gods of your birds,
your muses prophetic, whose words
all year round you've got,
unless it's too hot.
Your questions will always be heard.

And we won't run away to a cloud
and sit there like Zeus, who's so proud—
we're ready to give,
hang out where you live,
and be there for you in the crowd.

— ἀλλὰ παρόντες δώσομεν ὑμῖν
αὐτοῖς, παισίν, παίδων παισίν, 730
πλουθυγιείαν
εὐδαιμονίαν βίον εἰρήνην
νεότητα γέλωτα χοροὺς θαλίας
γάλα τ᾽ ὀρνίθων. ὥστε παρέσται
κοπιᾶν ὑμῖν ὑπὸ τῶν ἀγαθῶν· 735
οὕτω πλουτήσετε πάντες.

— Μοῦσα λοχμαία,
τιὸ τιὸ τιὸ τιὸ τιὸ τιὸ τιοτίγξ,
ποικίλη, μεθ᾽ ἧς ἐγὼ
νάπαισι καὶ κορυφαῖς ἐν ὀρείαις, 740
τιὸ τιὸ τιὸ τιοτίγξ,
ἱζόμενος μελίας ἐπὶ φυλλοκόμου,
τιὸ τιὸ τιὸ τιοτίγξ,
δι᾽ ἐμῆς γένυος ξουθῆς μελέων
Πανὶ νόμους ἱεροὺς ἀναφαίνω 745
σεμνά τε μητρὶ χορεύματ᾽ ὀρείᾳ,
τοτοτοτοτοτοτοτοτίγξ,
ἔνθεν ὡστερεὶ μέλιττα
Φρύνιχος ἀμβροσίων μελέων ἀπεβόσκετο καρπὸν ἀεὶ
φέρων γλυκεῖαν ᾠδάν. 750
τιὸ τιὸ τιὸ τιοτίγξ.

— εἰ μετ᾽ ὀρνίθων τις ὑμῶν ὦ θεαταὶ βούλεται
διαπλέκειν ζῶν ἡδέως τὸ λοιπόν, ὡς ἡμᾶς ἴτω.
ὅσα γάρ ἐστιν ἐνθάδ᾽ αἰσχρὰ τῷ νόμῳ κρατούμενα, 755
ταῦτα πάντ᾽ ἐστὶν παρ᾽ ἡμῖν τοῖσιν ὄρνισιν καλά.
εἰ γὰρ ἐνθάδ᾽ ἐστὶν αἰσχρὸν τὸν πατέρα τύπτειν νόμῳ,
τοῦτ᾽ ἐκεῖ καλὸν παρ᾽ ἡμῖν ἐστιν, ἤν τις τῷ πατρὶ
προσδραμὼν εἴπῃ πατάξας, ʿαἶρε πλῆκτρον, εἰ μαχεῖ.ʾ
εἰ δὲ τυγχάνει τις ὑμῶν δραπέτης ἐστιγμένος, 760
ἀτταγᾶς οὗτος παρ᾽ ἡμῖν ποικίλος κεκλήσεται.
εἰ δὲ τυγχάνει τις ὢν Φρὺξ μηδὲν ἧττον Σπινθάρου,
φρυγίλος ὄρνις ἐνθάδ᾽ ἔσται, τοῦ Φιλήμονος γένους.
εἰ δὲ δοῦλός ἐστι καὶ Κὰρ ὥσπερ Ἐξηκεστίδης,

CHORUS LEADER

Yes, to you, your children, and their children, too,   [730]
we'll grant wealth and health, good life, and happiness,
peace, youth, laughter, dances, festivals of song—
and birds' milk, too—so much, you'll find yourself worn out
with our fine gifts—yes, that's how rich you'll be.

CHORUS

O woodland Muse
    Tio-tio-tio-tiotinx
my muse of varied artful song
on trees and from high mountain peaks   [740]
    tio-tio-tio-tiotinx
to your notes I sing along
in my leafy ash tree seat.
    tio-tio-tio-tiontinx
From my tawny throat I fling
my sacred melodies to Pan.
In holy dance I chant and sing
our mother from the mountain land.
    Toto-toto-toto-toto-toto-totinx
Here Phrynichus would always sip   [750]
ambrosial nectar from our tone
to make sweet music of his own.
    tio-tio-tio-tiotinx.

CHORUS LEADER

If there's someone out there in the audience
who'd like to spend his future life among the birds
enjoying himself, he should come to us. Here, you see,
whatever is considered shameful by your laws,
is all just fine among us birds. Consider this—
if your tradition says one shouldn't beat one's dad,
up here with us it's all right if some young bird
goes at his father, hits him, cries, "You wanna fight?
Then put up your spur!" If out there among you all   [760]
there is, by chance, a tattooed slave who's run away,
we'll call him a spotted francolin. Or else,
if someone happens to be Phrygian, as pure
as Spintharos, he'll be a Philemon-bred finch.
If he's like Execestides, a Carian slave,

Aristophanes

φυσάτω πάππους παρ' ἡμῖν, καὶ φανοῦνται φράτερες. 765

εἰ δ' ὁ Πεισίου προδοῦναι τοῖς ἀτίμοις τὰς πύλας

βούλεται, πέρδιξ γενέσθω, τοῦ πατρὸς νεοττίον·

ὡς παρ' ἡμῖν οὐδὲν αἰσχρόν ἐστιν ἐκπερδικίσαι.

— τοιάδε κύκνοι,

τιὸ τιὸ τιὰ τιὸ τιὸ τιοτίγξ, 770

συμμιγῆ βοὴν ὁμοῦ

πτεροῖς κρέκοντες ἴακχον Ἀπόλλω,

τιὸ τιὸ τιὸ τιοτίγξ,

ὄχθῳ ἐφεζόμενοι παρ' Ἕβρον ποταμόν,

τιὸ τιὸ τιὸ τιοτίγξ, 775

διὰ δ' αἰθέριον νέφος ἦλθε βοά·

πτῆξε δὲ φῦλά τε ποικίλα θηρῶν,

κύματά τ' ἔσβεσε νήνεμος αἴθρη,

τοτοτοτοτοτοτοτοτίγξ·

πᾶς δ' ἐπεκτύπησ' Ὄλυμπος· 780

εἷλε δὲ θάμβος ἄνακτας· Ὀλυμπιάδες δὲ μέλος Χάριτες

Μοῦσαί τ' ἐπωλόλυξαν.

τιὸ τιὸ τιὸ τιοτίγξ.

— οὐδέν ἐστ' ἄμεινον οὐδ' ἥδιον ἢ φῦσαι πτερά. 785

αὐτίχ' ὑμῶν τῶν θεατῶν εἴ τις ἦν ὑπόπτερος,

εἶτα πεινῶν τοῖς χοροῖσι τῶν τραγῳδῶν ἤχθετο,

let him act the Cuckoo—steal his kin from us—
some group of citizens will claim him soon enough.
And if the son of Peisias still has in mind
betraying our city gates to worthless men,
let him become his father's little partridge cock—
for us there's nothing wrong with crafty partridge stock.

CHORUS

        Tio-tio-tio-tio-tinx-
        That's how the swans   [770]
        massed in a crowd
        with rustling wings
        once raised aloud
        Apollo's hymn.

        Tio-tio-tio-tio-tinx
        They sat in rows
        on river banks
        where Hebros flows.
        Tio-tio-tio-tio-tinx

        Their song then rose
        through cloud and air—
        it cast its spell
        on mottled tribes
        of wild beasts there—
        the silent sky
        calmed down the sea.
        Toto-toto-toto-toto-totinx.

        Olympus rang—   [780]
        amazement seized
        its lords and kings.
        Then Muses there
        and Graces, too,
        voiced their response—
        Olympus sang.
        Tio-tio-tio-tio-tiotinx.

CHORUS LEADER

There's nothing sweeter or better than growing wings.
If any of you members of the audience
had wings, well, if you were feeling bored or hungry
with these tragic choruses, you could fly away,

Aristophanes

ἐκπτόμενος ἂν οὗτος ἠρίστησεν ἐλθὼν οἴκαδε,
κᾆτ᾽ ἂν ἐμπλησθεὶς ἐφ᾽ ἡμᾶς αὖθις αὖ κατέπτετο.

εἴ τε Πατροκλείδης τις ὑμῶν τυγχάνει χεζητιῶν,   790
οὐκ ἂν ἐξίδισεν ἐς θοἰμάτιον, ἀλλ᾽ ἀνέπτετο,
κἀποπαρδὼν κἀναπνεύσας αὖθις αὖ κατέπτετο·
εἴ τε μοιχεύων τις ὑμῶν ἐστιν ὅστις τυγχάνει,
κᾆθ᾽ ὁρᾷ τὸν ἄνδρα τῆς γυναικὸς ἐν βουλευτικῷ,
οὗτος ἂν πάλιν παρ᾽ ὑμῶν πτερυγίσας ἀνέπτετο,   795
εἶτα βινήσας ἐκεῖθεν αὖθις αὖ κατέπτετο.
ἆρ᾽ ὑπόπτερον γενέσθαι παντός ἐστιν ἄξιον;
ὡς Διειτρέφης γε πυτιναῖα μόνον ἔχων πτερὰ
ᾑρέθη φύλαρχος, εἶθ᾽ ἵππαρχος, εἶτ᾽ ἐξ οὐδενὸς
μεγάλα πράττει κἀστὶ νυνὶ ξουθὸς ἱππαλεκτρυών.   800

ΠΙΣΘΕΤΑΙΡΟΣ
ταυτὶ τοιαυτί· μὰ Δί᾽ ἐγὼ μὲν πρᾶγμά πω
γελοιότερον οὐκ εἶδον οὐδεπώποτε.

ΕΥΕΛΠΙΔΗΣ
ἐπὶ τῷ γελᾷς;

ΠΙΣΘΕΤΑΙΡΟΣ
ἐπὶ τοῖσι σοῖς ὠκυπτέροις.
οἶσθ᾽ ᾧ μάλιστ᾽ ἔοικας ἐπτερωμένος;
εἰς εὐτέλειαν χηνὶ συγγεγραμμένῳ.   805

ΕΥΕΛΠΙΔΗΣ
σὺ δὲ κοψίχῳ γε σκάφιον ἀποτετιλμένῳ.

ΠΙΣΘΕΤΑΙΡΟΣ
ταυτὶ μὲν ᾐκάσμεσθα κατὰ τὸν Αἰσχύλον·
τάδ᾽ οὐχ ὑπ᾽ ἄλλων ἀλλὰ τοῖς αὐτῶν πτεροῖς.

ΧΟΡΟΣ
ἄγε δὴ τί χρὴ δρᾶν;

go home for dinner, and then, once you'd had enough,
fly back to us again. Or if, by any chance,
a Patrocleides sits out there among you all,   [790]
dying to shit, he wouldn't have to risk a fart
in his own pants—he could fly off and let 'er rip,
take a deep breath, and fly back down again.
If it should be the case that one of you out there
is having an affair, and you observe her husband
sitting here, in seats reserved for Council men,
well, once again, you could fly off and fuck the wife,
then fly back from her place and take your seat once more.
Don't you see how having wings to fly beats everything?
Just look at Diitrephes—the only wings he had
were handles on his flasks of wine, but nonetheless,
they chose him to lead a squad of cavalry,
then for a full command, so now, from being nobody,
he carries out our great affairs—he's now become   [800]
a tawny civic horse-cock.⁴⁵

[Enter Pisthetairos and Euelpides from Tereus' house. They now have wings on
and feathers on their heads instead of hair]

PISTHETAIROS
                    Well, that's that. By Zeus,
I've never seen a more ridiculous sight!

EUELPIDES
    What are you laughing at?

PISTHETAIROS
                    At your feathers.
Have you any idea what you look like—
what you most resemble with those feathers on?
A goose painted by some cheap artiste!

EUELPIDES
    And you look like a blackbird—one whose hair
    has just been cut using a barber's bowl.

PISTHETAIROS
    People will use us as metaphors—
    as Aeschlyus would say, "We're shot by feathers
    not from someone else but of our very own."

CHORUS LEADER
    All right, then. What do we now need to do?

ΠΙΣΘΕΤΑΙΡΟΣ

    πρῶτον ὄνομα τῇ πόλει
θέσθαι τι μέγα καὶ κλεινόν, εἶτα τοῖς θεοῖς   810
θῦσαι μετὰ τοῦτο.

ΕΥΕΛΠΙΔΗΣ

             ταῦτα κἀμοὶ συνδοκεῖ.

ΧΟΡΟΣ

φέρ' ἴδω, τί δ' ἡμῖν τοὔνομ' ἔσται τῇ πόλει;

ΕΥΕΛΠΙΔΗΣ

βούλεσθε τὸ μέγα τοῦτο τοὐκ Λακεδαίμονος
Σπάρτην ὄνομα καλῶμεν αὐτήν;

ΠΙΣΘΕΤΑΙΡΟΣ

                  Ἡράκλεις·
Σπάρτην γὰρ ἂν θείμην ἐγὼ τἠμῇ πόλει;   815
οὐδ' ἂν χαμεύνῃ πάνυ γε κειρίαν γ' ἔχων.

ΕΥΕΛΠΙΔΗΣ

τί δῆτ' ὄνομ' αὐτῇ θησόμεσθ';

ΧΟΡΟΣ

               ἐντευθενὶ
ἐκ τῶν νεφελῶν καὶ τῶν μετεώρων χωρίων
χαῦνόν τι πάνυ.

ΠΙΣΘΕΤΑΙΡΟΣ

          βούλει Νεφελοκοκκυγίαν;

ΧΟΡΟΣ

ἰοὺ ἰού·
καλόν γ' ἀτεχνῶς σὺ καὶ μέγ' ηὖρες τοὔνομα.   820

ΕΥΕΛΠΙΔΗΣ

ἆρ' ἐστὶν αὑτηγὶ Νεφελοκοκκυγία,
ἵνα καὶ τὰ Θεογένους τὰ πολλὰ χρήματα
τά τ' Αἰσχίνου γ' ἅπαντα;

ΠΙΣΘΕΤΑΙΡΟΣ

              καὶ λῷστον μὲν οὖν
τὸ Φλέγρας πεδίον, ἵν' οἱ θεοὶ τοὺς γηγενεῖς
ἀλαζονευόμενοι καθυπερηκόντισαν.   825

PISTHETAIROS
> First, we have to name our city, something
> fine and grand. Then after that we sacrifice   [810]
> an offering to the gods.

EUELPIDES
>   That's my view, too.

CHORUS LEADER
> So what name shall we give our city?

PISTHETAIROS
> Well, do you want to use that mighty name
> from Lacedaimon—shall we call it Sparta?

EUELPIDES
> By Hercules, would I use that name Sparta
> for my city? No. I wouldn't even try
> esparto grass to make my bed, not if
> I could use cords of linen.[46]

PISTHETAIROS
>   All right then, what name
> shall we provide?

CHORUS LEADER
>   Some name from around here—
> to do with clouds, with high places full of air,
> something really extra grand.

PISTHETAIROS
>   Well, then,
> how do you like this: Cloudcuckooland?

CHORUS LEADER
> Yes! That's good! You've come up with a name   [820]
> that's really wonderful—it's great!

EUELPIDES
>   Hang on,
> is this Cloudcuckooland the very spot
> where Theogenes keeps lots of money,
> and Aeschines hides all his assets?[47]

PISTHETAIROS
> It's even more than that—it's Phlegra Plain,
> the place where gods beat up on all the giants
> in a bragging match.[48]

95

ΕΥΕΛΠΙΔΗΣ
λιπαρὸν τὸ χρῆμα τῆς πόλεως. τίς δαὶ θεὸς
πολιοῦχος ἔσται; τῷ ξανοῦμεν τὸν πέπλον;

ΠΙΣΘΕΤΑΙΡΟΣ
τί δ' οὐκ Ἀθηναίαν ἐῶμεν Πολιάδα;

ΕΥΕΛΠΙΔΗΣ
καὶ πῶς ἂν ἔτι γένοιτ' ἂν εὔτακτος πόλις,
ὅπου θεὸς γυνὴ γεγονυῖα πανοπλίαν   830
ἔστηκ' ἔχουσα, Κλεισθένης δὲ κερκίδα;

ΠΙΣΘΕΤΑΙΡΟΣ
τίς δαὶ καθέξει τῆς πόλεως τὸ Πελαργικόν;

ΧΟΡΟΣ
ὄρνις ἀφ' ἡμῶν τοῦ γένους τοῦ Περσικοῦ,
ὅσπερ λέγεται δεινότατος εἶναι πανταχοῦ
Ἄρεως νεοττός.   835

ΕΥΕΛΠΙΔΗΣ
                    ὦ νεοττὲ δέσποτα·
ὡς δ' ὁ θεὸς ἐπιτήδειος οἰκεῖν ἐπὶ πετρῶν.

ΠΙΣΘΕΤΑΙΡΟΣ
ἄγε νυν σὺ μὲν βάδιζε πρὸς τὸν ἀέρα
καὶ τοῖσι τειχίζουσι παραδιακόνει,
χάλικας παραφόρει, πηλὸν ἀποδὺς ὄργασον,
λεκάνην ἀνένεγκε, κατάπεσ' ἀπὸ τῆς κλίμακος,   840
φύλακας κατάστησαι, τὸ πῦρ ἔγκρυπτ' ἀεί,
κωδωνοφορῶν περίτρεχε καὶ κάθευδ' ἐκεῖ·
κήρυκα δὲ πέμψον τὸν μὲν ἐς θεοὺς ἄνω,
ἕτερον δ' ἄνωθεν αὖ παρ' ἀνθρώπους κάτω,
κἀκεῖθεν αὖθις παρ' ἐμέ.   845

ΕΥΕΛΠΙΔΗΣ
                    σὺ δέ γ' αὐτοῦ μένων
οἴμωζε παρ' ἔμ'.

ΠΙΣΘΕΤΑΙΡΟΣ
                    ἴθ' ὦγάθ' οἷ πέμπω σ' ἐγώ.
οὐδὲν γὰρ ἄνευ σοῦ τῶνδ' ἃ λέγω πεπράξεται.

EUELPIDES

                    This fine metropolis!
O what a glittering thing this city is!
Now who should be the city's guardian god?
Who gets to wear the sacred robes we weave?

PISTHETAIROS

Why not let Athena do the guarding?

EUELPIDES

But how can we have a finely ordered state
where a female goddess stands there fully armed,   [830]
while Cleisthenes still fondles weaving shuttles.[49]

PISTHETAIROS

Well, who will hold our city's strong Storkade?

CHORUS LEADER

A bird among us of a Persian breed —
it's said to be the fiercest anywhere
of all the war god's chicks.

EUELPIDES

                    Some princely cocks?
They're just the gods to live among the rocks!

PISTHETAIROS *[to Euelpides]*

Come now, you must move up into the air,
and help the ones who're building up the wall —
hoist rubble for 'em, strip and mix the mortar,
haul up the hod, and then fall off the ladder.   [840]
Put guards in place, and keep all fires concealed.
Make your inspection rounds holding the bell.[50]
Go to sleep up there. Then send out heralds —
one to gods above, one down to men below.
And then come back from there to me.

EUELPIDES

                    And you?
You'll stay here? Well, to hell with you . . .

PISTHETAIROS

                    Hey, my friend,
you should go where I send you — without you
none of that work I mentioned will get done.

ἐγὼ δ' ἵνα θύσω τοῖσι καινοῖσιν θεοῖς,

τὸν ἱερέα πέμψοντα τὴν πομπὴν καλῶ.

παῖ παῖ, τὸ κανοῦν αἴρεσθε καὶ τὴν χέρνιβα.   850

ΧΟΡΟΣ

ὁμορροθῶ, συνθέλω,

συμπαραινέσας ἔχω

προσόδια μεγάλα σεμνὰ προσιέναι θεοῖσιν,

ἅμα δὲ προσέτι χάριτος ἕνεκα προβάτιόν τι θύειν.   855

ἴτω ἴτω δὲ Πυθιὰς βοὰ θεῷ,

συνᾳδέτω δὲ Χαῖρις ᾠδάν.

ΠΙΣΘΕΤΑΙΡΟΣ

παῦσαι σὺ φυσῶν. Ἡράκλεις τουτὶ τί ἦν;

τουτὶ μὰ Δί' ἐγὼ πολλὰ δὴ καὶ δείν' ἰδὼν   860

οὔπω κόρακ' εἶδον ἐμπεφορβειωμένον.

ἱερεῦ σὸν ἔργον, θῦε τοῖς καινοῖς θεοῖς.

ΙΕΡΕΥΣ

δράσω τάδ'. ἀλλὰ ποῦ 'στιν ὁ τὸ κανοῦν ἔχων;

εὔχεσθε τῇ Ἑστίᾳ τῇ ὀρνιθείῳ καὶ τῷ ἰκτίνῳ τῷ ἑστιούχῳ

καὶ ὄρνισιν Ὀλυμπίοις καὶ Ὀλυμπίῃσιπᾶσι καὶ πάσῃσιν—

ΠΙΣΘΕΤΑΙΡΟΣ

ὦ Σουνιέρακε χαῖρ' ἄναξ Πελαργικέ.

98

We need a sacrifice to these new gods.
I'll call a priest to organize the show.

*[Euelpides exits. Pisthetairos calls to the slaves through the doors of Tereus'
house]*

You, boy, pick up the basket, and you,
my lad, grab up the holy water.   [850]

*[Pisthetairos enters the house. As the Chorus sings, the slaves emerge and pre-
pare for the sacrifice. The Chorus is accompanied by a raven playing the pipes]*

CHORUS
I think it's good and I agree,
your notions here are fine with me,
a great big march with dancing throngs
and to the gods send holy songs,
and then their benefits to keep
we'll sacrifice a baby sheep—
let go our cry, the Pythian shout,
while Chaeris plays our chorus out.

*[The Raven plays erratically on the pipe. Pisthetairos comes out of the house.
He brings a priest with him, who is leading a small scrawny goat for the
sacrifice]*

PISTHETAIROS *[to the Raven]*
Stop blowing all that noise! By Hercules,
what's this? I've seen some strange things, heaven knows,   [860]
but never this—a raven with a pipe
shoved up his nose. Come on, priest, work your spell,
and sacrifice to these new gods as well.

PRIEST
I'll do it. But where's the basket-bearing boy?

[The slave appears with the basket]

Let us now pray to Hestia of the birds,[51]
and to the Kite that watches o'er the hearth,
to all Olympian birds and birdesses . . .

PISTHETAIROS *[to himself]*
O Hawk of Sunium, all hail to you,
Lord of the Sea . . .

ΙΕΡΕΥΣ

καὶ κύκνῳ Πυθίῳ καὶ Δηλίῳ καὶ Λητοῖ Ὀρτυγομήτρᾳ καὶ
Ἀρτέμιδι Ἀκαλανθίδι—

ΠΙΣΘΕΤΑΙΡΟΣ

οὐκέτι Κολαινὶς ἀλλ᾽ Ἀκαλανθὶς Ἄρτεμις.

ΙΕΡΕΥΣ

καὶ φρυγίλῳ Σαβαζίῳ καὶ στρούθῳ μεγάλῃ μητρὶ θεῶν καὶ
ἀνθρώπων—

ΠΙΣΘΕΤΑΙΡΟΣ

δέσποινα Κυβέλη, στροῦθε, μῆτερ Κλεοκρίτου.

ΙΕΡΕΥΣ

διδόναι Νεφελοκοκκυγιεῦσιν ὑγιείαν καὶ σωτηρίαν αὐτοῖσι
καὶ Χίοισι—

ΠΙΣΘΕΤΑΙΡΟΣ

Χίοισιν ἥσθην πανταχοῦ προσκειμένοις.   880

ΙΕΡΕΥΣ

καὶ ἥρωσιν ὄρνισι καὶ ἡρώων παισί, πορφυρίωνι καὶ
πελεκᾶντι καὶ πελεκίνῳ καὶ φλέξιδι καὶ τέτρακικαὶ ταῶνι
καὶ ἐλεᾷ καὶ βασκᾷ καὶ ἐλασᾷ καὶ ἐρωδιῷ καὶ καταρράκτῃ
καὶ μελαγκορύφῳ καὶ αἰγιθάλλῳ—

ΠΙΣΘΕΤΑΙΡΟΣ

παῦ᾽ ἐς κόρακας, παῦσαι καλῶν. ἰοὺ ἰού,
ἐπὶ ποῖον ὦ κακόδαιμον ἱερεῖον καλεῖς   890
ἁλιαιέτους καὶ γῦπας; οὐχ ὁρᾷς ὅτι
ἰκτῖνος εἷς ἂν τοῦτό γ᾽ οἴχοιθ᾽ ἁρπάσας;
ἄπελθ᾽ ἀφ᾽ ἡμῶν καὶ σὺ καὶ τὰ στέμματα·
ἐγὼ γὰρ αὐτὸς τουτογὶ θύσω μόνος.

PRIEST

And to the Pythian Swan of Delos— [870]
let's pray to Leto, mother of the quail
to Artemis the Goldfinch . . .

PISTHETAIROS

Ha! No more goddess
of Colaenis now, but goldfinch Artemis . . .

PRIEST

. . . to Sabazdios, Phrygian frigate bird,
to the great ostrich mother of the gods
and of all men . . .

PISTHETAIROS

. . . to Cybele, our ostrich queen,
mother of Cleocritos[52] . . .

PRIEST

. . . may they give
to all Cloudcuckooites security,
good health, as well—and to the Chians, too.[53]

PISTHETAIROS

I do like that—the way those Chians [880]
always get tacked on everywhere—

PRIEST

. . . to Hero birds, and to their chicks,
to Porphyrions and Pelicans,
both white and grey, to Raptor-birds and Pheasants,
Peacocks and Warblers . . .

[The Priest starts to get carried away]

. . . Ospreys and Teals
Herons and Gannets, Terns, small Tits, big Tits, and . . .

PISTHETAIROS *[interrupting]*

Hold on, dammit—stop calling all these birds.
You idiot! In what sort of sacrifice [890]
does one call for ospreys and for vultures?
Don't you see—one kite could snatch this goat,
then carry it away? Get out of here,
you and your garlands, too. I'll do it myself—
I'll offer up this beast all on my own.

ΧΟΡΟΣ
εἶτ᾽ αὖθις αὖ τἄρα σοι
δεῖ με δεύτερον μέλος
χέρνιβι θεοσεβὲς ὅσιον ἐπιβοᾶν, καλεῖν δὲ
μάκαρας, ἕνα τινὰ μόνον, εἴπερ ἱκανὸν ἕξετ᾽ ὄψον. 900
τὰ γὰρ παρόντα θύματ᾽ οὐδὲν ἄλλο πλὴν
γένειόν ἐστι καὶ κέρατα.

ΠΙΣΘΕΤΑΙΡΟΣ
θύοντες εὐξώμεσθα τοῖς πτερίνοις θεοῖς.

ΠΟΙΗΤΗΣ
Νεφελοκοκκυγίαν τὰν εὐδαίμονα
κλῇσον ὦ Μοῦσα τεαῖς ἐν ὕμνων ἀοιδαῖς. 905

ΠΙΣΘΕΤΑΙΡΟΣ
τουτὶ τὸ πρᾶγμα ποδαπόν; εἰπέ μοι τίς εἶ;

ΠΟΙΗΤΗΣ
ἐγὼ μελιγλώσσων ἐπέων ἱεὶς ἀοιδὰν
Μουσάων θεράπων ὀτρηρός,
κατὰ τὸν Ὅμηρον. 910

ΠΙΣΘΕΤΑΙΡΟΣ
ἔπειτα δῆτα δοῦλος ὢν κόμην ἔχεις;

ΠΟΙΗΤΗΣ
οὔκ, ἀλλὰ πάντες ἐσμὲν οἱ διδάσκαλοι
Μουσάων θεράποντες ὀτρηροί,
κατὰ τὸν Ὅμηρον.

ΠΙΣΘΕΤΑΙΡΟΣ
οὐκ ἐτὸς ὀτρηρὸν καὶ τὸ ληδάριον ἔχεις. 915
ἀτὰρ ὦ ποιητὰ κατὰ τί δεῦρ᾽ ἀνεφθάρης;

ΠΟΙΗΤΗΣ
μέλη πεποίηκ᾽ ἐς τὰς Νεφελοκοκκυγίας
τὰς ὑμετέρας κύκλιά τε πολλὰ καὶ καλὰ
καὶ παρθένεια καὶ κατὰ τὰ Σιμωνίδου.

[Pisthetairos pushes the Priest away. Exit Priest]

CHORUS

Now once again I have to sing
a song to purify you all,
a holy sacred melody.
The Blessed Ones I have to call—
but if you're in a mood to eat
we just need one and not a score
for here our sacrificial meat   [900]
is horns and hair, and nothing more.

PISTHETAIROS

Let us pray while we make sacrifice
to our feathery gods . . . *[raises his eyes to sky and shuts his eyes]*

[A poet suddenly bursts on the scene reciting his verses as he enters]

POET *[reciting]*

O Muse, in your songs sing the renown
of Cloudcuckooland—this happy town . . .

PISTHETAIROS

Where'd this thing come from? Tell me—who are you?

POET

Me? I'm a sweet tongued warbler of the words—
a nimble servant of the Muse, as Homer says.   [910]

PISTHETAIROS

You're a slave and wear your hair that long?

POET

No, but all poets of dramatic songs
are nimble servants of the Muse, as Homer says.

PISTHETAIROS

No doubt that's why your nimble cloak's so thin.
But, oh poet, why has thou come hither?

POET

I've been making up all sorts of splendid songs
to celebrate your fine Cloudcuckoolands—
dithyrambs and virgin songs and other tunes
after the style of that Simonides.⁵⁴

Aristophanes

ΠΙΣΘΕΤΑΙΡΟΣ
ταυτὶ σὺ πότ᾽ ἐποίησας; ἀπὸ ποίου χρόνου;   920

ΠΟΙΗΤΗΣ
πάλαι πάλαι δὴ τήνδ᾽ ἐγὼ κλῄζω πόλιν.

ΠΙΣΘΕΤΑΙΡΟΣ
οὐκ ἄρτι θύω τὴν δεκάτην ταύτης ἐγώ,
καὶ τοὔνομ᾽ ὥσπερ παιδίῳ νῦν δὴ ᾽θέμην;

ΠΟΙΗΤΗΣ
ἀλλά τις ὠκεῖα Μουσάων φάτις
οἷάπερ ἵππων ἀμαρυγά.   925
σὺ δὲ πάτερ κτίστορ Αἴτνας,
ζαθέων ἱερῶν ὁμώνυμε,
δὸς ἐμὶν ὅ τι περ
τεᾷ κεφαλᾷ θέλῃς
πρόφρων δόμεν ἐμὶν τεΐν.   930

ΠΙΣΘΕΤΑΙΡΟΣ
τουτὶ παρέξει τὸ κακὸν ἡμῖν πράγματα,
εἰ μή τι τούτῳ δόντες ἀποφευξούμεθα.
οὗτος, σὺ μέντοι σπολάδα καὶ χιτῶν᾽ ἔχεις,
ἀπόδυθι καὶ δὸς τῷ ποιητῇ τῷ σοφῷ.
ἔχε τὴν σπολάδα· πάντως δέ μοι ῥιγῶν δοκεῖς.   935

ΠΟΙΗΤΗΣ
τόδε μὲν οὐκ ἀέκουσα φίλα
Μοῦσα δῶρον δέχεται·
τὺ δὲ τεᾷ φρενὶ μάθε Πινδάρειον ἔπος —

ΠΙΣΘΕΤΑΙΡΟΣ
ἄνθρωπος ἡμῶν οὐκ ἀπαλλαχθήσεται.   940

ΠΟΙΗΤΗΣ
νομάδεσσι γὰρ ἐν Σκύθαις
ἀλᾶται Στράτων,
ὃς ὑφαντοδόνατον ἔσθος οὐ πέπαται·
ἀκλεὴς δ᾽ ἔβα σπολὰς ἄνευ χιτῶνος.
ξύνες ὅ τοι λέγω.   945

PISTHETAIROS
  When did you compose these tunes? Some time ago?   [920]

POET
  O long long ago—yes, I've been singing
  the glory of this town for years.

PISTHETAIROS
                    Look here—
  I've just been making sacrifice today—
  the day our city gets its name. What's more,
  it's only now, as with a new-born child,
  I've given it that name.

POET
  Ah yes, but Muses' words are swift indeed—
  like twinkling hooves on rapid steeds.
  So thou, oh father, first of Aetna's kings,
  whose name means lots of holy things,
  present me something from thy grace
  whate'er you wish, just nod your face.[55]   [930]

PISTHETAIROS
  This fellow here is going to give us trouble—
  unless we can escape by giving something.

[Calling one of the slaves]

  You there with the tunic and the jerkin on.
  Strip off the leather jerkin. Give it up
  to this master poet. Take this jerkin.
  You look as if you're really freezing cold.

POET
  The darling Muse accepts the gift
  and not unwillingly—
  But now your wit should get a lift
  from Pindar's words which . . .

PISTHETAIROS
  This fellow's never going to go away!   [940]

POET *[making up a quotation]*
  "Out there amid nomadic Scythians,
  he wanders from the host in all his shame,
  he who has no woven garment shuttle-made—
  a jerkin on, but no tunic to his name."
  I speak so you can understand.

ΠΙΣΘΕΤΑΙΡΟΣ
ξυνῆχ᾽ ὅτι βούλει τὸν χιτωνίσκον λαβεῖν.
ἀπόδυθι· δεῖ γὰρ τὸν ποιητὴν ὠφελεῖν.
ἄπελθε τουτονὶ λαβών.

ΠΟΙΗΤΗΣ
ἀπέρχομαι,
κἀς τὴν πόλιν γ᾽ ἐλθὼν ποιήσω τοιαδί·
'κλῇσον ὦ χρυσόθρονε τὰν τρομερὰν κρυεράν·   950
νιφόβολα πεδία πολύπορά τ᾽ ἤλυθον ἀλαλάν.'

ΠΙΣΘΕΤΑΙΡΟΣ
νὴ τὸν Δί᾽ ἀλλ᾽ ἤδη πέφευγας ταυταγὶ
τὰ κρυερὰ τονδὶ τὸν χιτωνίσκον λαβών.   955
τουτὶ μὰ Δί᾽ ἐγὼ τὸ κακὸν οὐδέποτ᾽ ἤλπισα,
οὕτω ταχέως τοῦτον πεπύσθαι τὴν πόλιν.
αὖθις σὺ περιχώρει λαβὼν τὴν χέρνιβα.
εὐφημία 'στω.

ΧΡΗΣΜΟΛΟΓΟΣ
μὴ κατάρξῃ τοῦ τράγου.

ΠΙΣΘΕΤΑΙΡΟΣ
σὺ δ᾽ εἶ τίς;   960

ΧΡΗΣΜΟΛΟΓΟΣ
ὅστις; χρησμολόγος.

ΠΙΣΘΕΤΑΙΡΟΣ
οἴμωζέ νυν.

ΧΡΗΣΜΟΛΟΓΟΣ
ὦ δαιμόνιε τὰ θεῖα μὴ φαύλως φέρε·
ὡς ἔστι Βάκιδος χρησμὸς ἄντικρυς λέγων
ἐς τὰς Νεφελοκοκκυγίας.

106

PISTHETAIROS
Yes, I get it—you want the tunic, too.
[To the slave] Take it off. We must assist our poets.
Take it and get out.

POET
                    I'm on my way—
But as I go I'll still make songs like these
in honour of your city—
"O thou sitting on a golden throne,   [950]
sing to celebrate that shivering, quivering land.
I walked its snow-swept fruitful plains . . ."

[At this point Pisthetairos has had enough. He grabs the poet and throws him into the wings]

POET *[as he exits]*
                    Aaaaiiiii!

PISTHETAIROS *[calling after him]*
Well, by Zeus, at least you've now put behind
the cold, since you've got that little tunic on!
God knows, that's a problem I'd not thought about—
he learned about our city here so fast.
[resuming the sacrifice] Come, boy, pick up the holy water
and walk around again. Let everyone
observe a sacred holy silence now . . .

[Enter an Oracle Monger, quickly interrupting the ceremony. He is carrying a scroll]

ORACLE MONGER
Don't sacrifice that goat!

PISTHETAIROS
                    What? Who are you?

ORACLE MONGER
Who am I? I'm an oracular interpreter.

PISTHETAIROS
To hell with you!   [960]

ORACLE MONGER
                    Now, now, my dear good man,
don't disparage things divine. You should know
there's an oracle of Bacis which speaks
of your Cloudcuckooland—it's pertinent.

ΠΙΣΘΕΤΑΙΡΟΣ

κἄπειτα πῶς

ταῦτ᾽ οὐκ ἐχρησμολόγεις σὺ πρὶν ἐμὲ τὴν πόλιν

τήνδ᾽ οἰκίσαι; 965

ΧΡΗΣΜΟΛΟΓΟΣ

τὸ θεῖον ἐνεπόδιζέ με.

ΠΙΣΘΕΤΑΙΡΟΣ

ἀλλ᾽ οὐδὲν οἷόν ἐστ᾽ ἀκοῦσαι τῶν ἐπῶν.

ΧΡΗΣΜΟΛΟΓΟΣ

ἀλλ᾽ ὅταν οἰκήσωσι λύκοι πολιαί τε κορῶναι

ἐν ταὐτῷ τὸ μεταξὺ Κορίνθου καὶ Σικυῶνος,—

ΠΙΣΘΕΤΑΙΡΟΣ

τί οὖν προσήκει δῆτ᾽ ἐμοὶ Κορινθίων;

ΧΡΗΣΜΟΛΟΓΟΣ

ἠνίξαθ᾽ ὁ Βάκις τοῦτο πρὸς τὸν ἀέρα. 970

πρῶτον Πανδώρᾳ θῦσαι λευκότριχα κριόν·

ὃς δέ κ᾽ ἐμῶν ἐπέων ἔλθῃ πρώτιστα προφήτης,

τῷ δόμεν ἱμάτιον καθαρὸν καὶ καινὰ πέδιλα—

ΠΙΣΘΕΤΑΙΡΟΣ

ἔνεστι καὶ τὰ πέδιλα;

ΧΡΗΣΜΟΛΟΓΟΣ

λαβὲ τὸ βιβλίον.

καὶ φιάλην δοῦναι, καὶ σπλάγχνων χεῖρ᾽ ἐπιπλῆσαι. 975

ΠΙΣΘΕΤΑΙΡΟΣ

καὶ σπλάγχνα διδόν᾽ ἔνεστι;

ΧΡΗΣΜΟΛΟΓΟΣ

λαβὲ τὸ βιβλίον.

κἂν μὲν θέσπιε κοῦρε ποιῇς ταῦθ᾽ ὡς ἐπιτέλλω,

αἰετὸς ἐν νεφέλῃσι γενήσεαι· αἰ δέ κε μὴ δῷς,

οὐκ ἔσει οὐ τρυγὼν οὐδ᾽ αἰετὸς οὐ δρυκολάπτης.

ΠΙΣΘΕΤΑΙΡΟΣ

καὶ ταῦτ᾽ ἔνεστ᾽ ἐνταῦθα; 980

PISTHETAIROS

Then how come you didn't talk to me
about this prophecy some time before
I set my city here?

ORACLE MONGER

I could not do that—
powers divine held me in check.

PISTHETAIROS

Well, I guess
there's nothing wrong in listening to it now.

ORACLE MONGER *[unrolling the scroll and reading from it]*
"Once grey crows and wolves shall live together
in that space between Corinth and Sicyon . . ."

PISTHETAIROS

What my connection to Corinthians?

ORACLE MONGER

Its Bacis' cryptic way of saying "air." [970]
"First sacrifice to Pandora a white-fleeced ram.
Whoever first comes to prophesy my words,
let him receive a brand new cloak and sandals."

PISTHETAIROS

Are sandals in there, too?

ORACLE MONGER *[showing the scroll]*

Consult the book.
"Give him the bowl, fill his hands full with offal . . ."

PISTHETAIROS

The entrails? Does it says that in there?

ORACLE MONGER

Consult the book. "Inspired youth,
if thou dost complete what here I do command,
thou shalt become an eagle in the clouds—if not,
if thou will not give them me, you'll ne'er become
an eagle, or a turtle dove, or woodpecker."

PISTHETAIROS

That's all in there, as well?

ΧΡΗΣΜΟΛΟΓΟΣ

Aristophanes

λαβὲ τὸ βιβλίον.

ΠΙΣΘΕΤΑΙΡΟΣ

οὐδὲν ἄρ' ὅμοιός ἐσθ' ὁ χρησμὸς τουτῳί,
ὃν ἐγὼ παρὰ τἀπόλλωνος ἐξεγραψάμην·
αὐτὰρ ἐπὴν ἄκλητος ἰὼν ἄνθρωπος ἀλαζὼν
λυπῇ θύοντας καὶ σπλαγχνεύειν ἐπιθυμῇ,
δὴ τότε χρὴ τύπτειν αὐτὸν πλευρῶν τὸ μεταξὺ —   985

ΧΡΗΣΜΟΛΟΓΟΣ

οὐδὲν λέγειν οἶμαί σε.

ΠΙΣΘΕΤΑΙΡΟΣ

λαβὲ τὸ βιβλίον.
καὶ φείδου μηδὲν μηδ' αἰετοῦ ἐν νεφέλῃσιν,
μήτ' ἢν Λάμπων ᾖ μήτ' ἢν ὁ μέγας Διοπείθης.

ΧΡΗΣΜΟΛΟΓΟΣ

καὶ ταῦτ' ἔνεστ' ἐνταῦθα;

ΠΙΣΘΕΤΑΙΡΟΣ

λαβὲ τὸ βιβλίον.
οὐκ εἶ θύραζ'; ἐς κόρακας.

ΧΡΗΣΜΟΛΟΓΟΣ

οἴμοι δείλαιος.   990

ΠΙΣΘΕΤΑΙΡΟΣ

οὔκουν ἑτέρωσε χρησμολογήσεις ἐκτρέχων;

ΜΕΤΩΝ

ἥκω παρ' ὑμᾶς —

ΠΙΣΘΕΤΑΙΡΟΣ

ἕτερον αὖ τουτὶ κακόν.
τί δ' αὖ σὺ δράσων; τίς δ' ἰδέα βουλεύματος;
τίς ἡ 'πίνοια, τίς ὁ κόθορνος τῆς ὁδοῦ;

ORACLE MONGER

> Consult the book. [980]

PISTHETAIROS *[pulling out a sheet of paper from under his tunic]*
Your oracle is not at all like this one—
Apollo's very words. I them wrote down.
"When an impostor comes without an invitation—
a cheating rogue—and pesters men at sacrifice,
so keen is he to taste the inner parts, well then,
he must be beaten hard between the ribs . . ."

ORACLE MONGER
I don't think you're reading that.

PISTHETAIROS

> Consult the book.
"Do not spare him, even if he's way up there,
an eagle in the clouds, or if he's Lampon
or great Diopeithes in the flesh."[56]

ORACLE MONGER
That's not in there, is it?

PISTHETAIROS

> Consult the book.
Now, get out! To hell with you . . .

{Pisthetairos beats the Oracle Monger off stage, hitting him with the scroll]

ORACLE MONGER

> Ooooh . . . poor me! *[Exit]* [990]

PISTHETAIROS
Run off and do your soothsaying somewhere else!

[Enter Meton, carrying various surveying instruments, and wearing soft leather buskin boots][57]

METON
I have come here among you all . . .

PISTHETAIROS

> Here's more trouble.
And what have *you* come here to do? Your scheme—
what's it look like? What do you have in mind?
Why hike up here in buskin?

ΜΕΤΩΝ

γεωμετρῆσαι βούλομαι τὸν ἀέρα   995
ὑμῖν διελεῖν τε κατὰ γύας.

ΠΙΣΘΕΤΑΙΡΟΣ

προς τῶν θεῶν
σὺ δ᾽ εἶ τίς ἀνδρῶν;

ΜΕΤΩΝ

ὅστις εἴμ᾽ ἐγώ; Μέτων,
ὃν οἶδεν Ἑλλὰς χὠ Κολωνός.

ΠΙΣΘΕΤΑΙΡΟΣ

εἰπέ μοι,
ταυτὶ δέ σοι τί ἔστι;

ΜΕΤΩΝ

κανόνες ἀέρος.
αὐτίκα γὰρ ἀήρ ἐστι τὴν ἰδέαν ὅλος   1000
κατὰ πνιγέα μάλιστα. προσθεὶς οὖν ἐγὼ
τὸν κανόν᾽, ἄνωθεν τουτονὶ τὸν καμπύλον
ἐνθεὶς διαβήτην—μανθάνεις;

ΠΙΣΘΕΤΑΙΡΟΣ

οὐ μανθάνω.

ΜΕΤΩΝ

ὀρθῷ μετρήσω κανόνι προστιθείς, ἵνα
ὁ κύκλος γένηται σοι τετράγωνος κἀν μέσῳ   1005
ἀγορά, φέρουσαι δ᾽ ὦσιν εἰς αὐτὴν ὁδοὶ
ὀρθαὶ πρὸς αὐτὸ τὸ μέσον, ὥσπερ δ᾽ ἀστέρος
αὐτοῦ κυκλοτεροῦς ὄντος ὀρθαὶ πανταχῇ
ἀκτῖνες ἀπολάμπωσιν.

ΠΙΣΘΕΤΑΙΡΟΣ

ἄνθρωπος Θαλῆς.
Μέτων—   1010

ΜΕΤΩΝ

τί ἔστιν;

112

METON

> I intend
> to measure out the air for you—dividing it
> in surveyed lots.

PISTHETAIROS

> For heaven's sake,
> who are you?

METON *[shocked]*

> Who am I? I'm Meton—
> famous throughout Greece and Colonus.[58]

PISTHETAIROS

> What are these things you've got?

METON

> Rods to measure air.
> You see, the air is, in its totality,   [1000]
> shaped like a domed pot cover . . . Thus . . . and so,
> from up above I'll lay my ruler . . . it bends . . . thus . . .
> set my compass inside there . . . You see?

PISTHETAIROS

> I don't get it.

METON

> With this straight ruler here
> I measure this, so that your circle here
> becomes a square—and right in the middle there
> we have a market place, with straight highways
> proceeding to the centre, like a star,
> which, although circular, shines forth straight beams
> in all directions . . . Thus . . .

PISTHETAIROS

> This man's a Thales[59]
> Now, Meton . . .

METON

> What?

ΠΙΣΘΕΤΑΙΡΟΣ

οἶσθ' ὁτιὴ φιλῶ σ' ἐγώ,
κἀμοὶ πιθόμενος ὑπαποκίνει τῆς ὁδοῦ.

ΜΕΤΩΝ

τί δ' ἐστὶ δεινόν;

ΠΙΣΘΕΤΑΙΡΟΣ

ὥσπερ ἐν Λακεδαίμονι
ξενηλατοῦνται καὶ κεκίνηνταί τινες·
πληγαὶ συχναὶ κατ' ἄστυ.

ΜΕΤΩΝ

μῶν στασιάζετε;

ΠΙΣΘΕΤΑΙΡΟΣ

μὰ τὸν Δί' οὐ δῆτ'.   1015

ΜΕΤΩΝ

ἀλλὰ πῶς;

ΠΙΣΘΕΤΑΙΡΟΣ

ὁμοθυμαδὸν
σποδεῖν ἅπαντας τοὺς ἀλαζόνας δοκεῖ.

ΜΕΤΩΝ

ὑπάγοιμί τἄρ' ἄν.

ΠΙΣΘΕΤΑΙΡΟΣ

νὴ Δί' ὡς οὐκ οἶδ' ἂν εἰ
φθαίης ἄν· ἐπίκεινται γὰρ ἐγγὺς αὐταί.

ΜΕΤΩΝ

οἴμοι κακοδαίμων.

ΠΙΣΘΕΤΑΙΡΟΣ

οὐκ ἔλεγον ἐγὼ πάλαι;
οὐκ ἀναμετρήσεις σαυτὸν ἀπιὼν ἀλλαχῇ;   1020

ἘΠΙΣΚΟΠΟΣ

ποῦ πρόξενοι;

ΠΙΣΘΕΤΑΙΡΟΣ

τίς ὁ Σαρδανάπαλλος οὑτοσί;

Birds

PISTHETAIROS

You know I love you—   [1010]
so do as I say and head out of town.

METON
Am I in peril?

PISTHETAIROS

It's like in Sparta—
they're kicking strangers out—lots of trouble—
plenty of beatings on the way through town.

METON
You mean a revolution?

PISTHETAIROS

God no, not that.

METON
Then what?

PISTHETAIROS

They've reached a firm decision—
it was unanimous—to punch out every quack.

METON
I think I'd best be off.

PISTHETAIROS

You should, by god,
although you may not be in time—the blows
are coming thick and fast . . .

[Pisthetairos starts hitting Meton]

METON *[running off]*

O dear me . . . I'm in a pickle.

[Exit Meton. Pisthetairos yells after him]

PISTHETAIROS
Didn't I say that some time ago?
Go somewhere else and do your measuring!   [1020]

[Enter an Athenian Commissioner. He is carrying voting urns. He is dressed in an extravagantly official costume][60]

COMMISSIONER
Where are your honorary governors?

PISTHETAIROS
Who is this man—a Sardanapallos?[61]

115

Aristophanes

ΕΠΙΣΚΟΠΟΣ
ἐπίσκοπος ἥκω δεῦρο τῷ κυάμῳ λαχὼν
ἐς τὰς Νεφελοκοκκυγίας.

ΠΙΣΘΕΤΑΙΡΟΣ
ἐπίσκοπος;
ἔπεμψε δὲ τίς σε δεῦρο;

ΕΠΙΣΚΟΠΟΣ
φαῦλον βιβλίον
Τελέου.   1025

ΠΙΣΘΕΤΑΙΡΟΣ
τί; βούλει δῆτα τὸν μισθὸν λαβὼν
μὴ πράγματ᾽ ἔχειν ἀλλ᾽ ἀπιέναι;

ΕΠΙΣΚΟΠΟΣ
νὴ τοὺς θεούς.
ἐκκλησιάσαι δ᾽ οὖν ἐδεόμην οἴκοι μένων.
ἔστιν γὰρ ἃ δι᾽ ἐμοῦ πέπρακται Φαρνάκῃ.

ΠΙΣΘΕΤΑΙΡΟΣ
ἄπιθι λαβών· ἔστιν δ᾽ ὁ μισθὸς οὑτοσί.

ΕΠΙΣΚΟΠΟΣ
τουτὶ τί ἦν;   1030

ΠΙΣΘΕΤΑΙΡΟΣ
ἐκκλησία περὶ Φαρνάκου.

ΕΠΙΣΚΟΠΟΣ
μαρτύρομαι τυπτόμενος ὢν ἐπίσκοπος.

ΠΙΣΘΕΤΑΙΡΟΣ
οὐκ ἀποσοβήσεις; οὐκ ἀποίσεις τὼ κάδω;
οὐ δεινά; καὶ πέμπουσιν ἤδη ᾽πισκόπους
ἐς τὴν πόλιν, πρὶν καὶ τεθύσθαι τοῖς θεοῖς;

116

COMMISSIONER

I have come here to Cloudcuckooland
as your Commissioner—I was picked by lot.

PISTHETAIROS

As Commissioner? Who sent you here?

COMMISSIONER

Some dreadful paper from that Teleas.[62]

PISTHETAIROS

How'd you like to receive your salary
and leave, without doing anything?

COMMISSIONER

By god,
that would be nice. I should be staying at home
for the assembly. I've been doing some work
on Pharnakes' behalf.[63]

PISTHETAIROS

Then take your fee
and go. Here's what you get . . . *[strikes him]*

COMMISSIONER

What was that?

PISTHETAIROS

A motion on behalf of Pharnakes.   [1030]

[Pisthetairos strikes him again]

COMMISSIONER

I call on witnesses—he's hitting me—
He can't do that—I'm a Commissioner!

[Exit the Commissioner, on the run. Pisthetairos chases him]

PISTHETAIROS

Piss off! And take your voting urns with you!
Don't you find it weird? Already they've sent out
Commissioners to oversee the city,
before we've made the gods a sacrifice.

[Enter a Statute-Seller reading from a long scroll]

ΨΗΦΙΣΜΑΤΟΠΩΛΗΣ

ἐὰν δ' ὁ Νεφελοκοκκυγιεὺς τὸν Ἀθηναῖον ἀδικῇ —   1035

ΠΙΣΘΕΤΑΙΡΟΣ

τουτὶ τί ἔστιν αὖ κακὸν τὸ βιβλίον;

ΨΗΦΙΣΜΑΤΟΠΩΛΗΣ

ψηφισματοπώλης εἰμὶ καὶ νόμους νέους
ἥκω παρ' ὑμᾶς δεῦρο πωλήσων.

ΠΙΣΘΕΤΑΙΡΟΣ

τὸ τί;

ΨΗΦΙΣΜΑΤΟΠΩΛΗΣ

χρῆσθαι Νεφελοκοκκυγιᾶς τοῖσδε τοῖς μέτροισι καὶ
σταθμοῖσι καὶ ψηφίσμασι καθάπερ Ὀλοφύξιοι.   1040

ΠΙΣΘΕΤΑΙΡΟΣ

σὺ δέ γ' οἶσπερ ὠτοτύξιοι χρήσει τάχα.

ΨΗΦΙΣΜΑΤΟΠΩΛΗΣ

οὗτος τί πάσχεις;

ΠΙΣΘΕΤΑΙΡΟΣ

οὐκ ἀποίσεις τοὺς νόμους;
πικροὺς ἐγώ σοι τήμερον δείξω νόμους.   1045

ΕΠΙΣΚΟΠΟΣ

καλοῦμαι Πισθέταιρον ὕβρεως ἐς τὸν Μουνιχιῶνα μῆνα.

ΠΙΣΘΕΤΑΙΡΟΣ

ἄληθες οὗτος; ἔτι γὰρ ἐνταῦθ' ἦσθα σύ;

ΨΗΦΙΣΜΑΤΟΠΩΛΗΣ

ἐὰν δέ τις ἐξελαύνῃ τοὺς ἄρχοντας καὶ μὴ δέχηται κατὰ
τὴν στήλην —   1050

STATUTE SELLER
"If a resident of Cloudcuckooland
should wrong a citizen of Athens . . ."

PISTHETAIROS
Here come scrolls again — what's the trouble now?

STATUTE SELLER
I'm a statute seller — and I've come here
to sell you brand-new laws.

PISTHETAIROS
What laws?

STATUTE SELLER
Like this —
"Residents of Cloudcuckooland must use   [1040]
the same weights and measures and currency
as those in Olophyxia."[64]

PISTHETAIROS [*kicking him in the bum*]
Soon enough
you'll use them on your ass, you Fix-your-Holean!!

STATUTE SELLER
What's up with you?

PISTHETAIROS
Take your laws and shove off!
Today I'll give you laws you really feel!

[*Statute Seller runs off. The Commissioner enters from the other side, behind Pisthetairos*]

COMMISSIONER [*reading from a paper*]
"I summon Pisthetairos to appear in court
in April on a charge of official outrage . . ."

PISTHETAIROS [*turning*]
Really? You again! Why are you still here?

[*Pisthetairos chases the Commissioner off again. The Statute Seller then re-appears on the other side, also reading from a paper*]

STATUTE SELLER
"If anyone chases off court officers
and won't receive them as the law decrees . . ."   [1050]

ΠΙΣΘΕΤΑΙΡΟΣ

οἴμοι κακοδαίμων, καὶ σὺ γὰρ ἐνταῦθ᾽ ἦσθ᾽ ἔτι;

ἘΠΙΣΚΟΠΟΣ

ἀπολῶ σε καὶ γράφω σε μυρίας δραχμάς.

ΠΙΣΘΕΤΑΙΡΟΣ

ἐγὼ δὲ σοῦ γε τὼ κάδω διασκεδῶ.

ΨΗΦΙΣΜΑΤΟΠΩΛΗΣ

μέμνησ᾽ ὅτε τῆς στήλης κατετίλας ἑσπέρας;

ΠΙΣΘΕΤΑΙΡΟΣ

αἰβοῖ· λαβέτω τις αὐτόν. οὗτος οὐ μενεῖς;   1055
ἀπίωμεν ἡμεῖς ὡς τάχιστ᾽ ἐντευθενὶ
θύσοντες εἴσω τοῖς θεοῖσι τὸν τράγον.

ΧΟΡΟΣ

ἤδη ᾽μοὶ τῷ παντόπτᾳ
καὶ παντάρχᾳ θνητοὶ πάντες
θύσουσ᾽ εὐκταίαις εὐχαῖς.   1060
πᾶσαν μὲν γὰρ γᾶν ὀπτεύω,
σῴζω δ᾽ εὐθαλεῖς καρποὺς
κτείνων παμφύλων γένναν
θηρῶν, ἃ πάντ᾽ ἐν γαίᾳ
ἐκ κάλυκος αὐξανόμενον γένυσι παμφάγοις   1065
δένδρεσί τ᾽ ἐφημένα καρπὸν ἀποβόσκεται·
κτείνω δ᾽ οἳ κήπους εὐώδεις
φθείρουσιν λύμαις ἐχθίσταις,
ἑρπετά τε καὶ δάκετα πάνθ᾽ ὅσαπερ
ἔστιν ὑπ᾽ ἐμᾶς πτέρυγος ἐν φοναῖς ὄλλυται.   1070

PISTHETAIROS *[turning]*
This is getting really bad—you still here?

[Pisthetairos chases off the Statute Seller. The Commissioner re-appears on the other side of the stage]

COMMISSIONER
I'll ruin you! I'll take you to court—
ten thousand drachmas you'll . . .

PISTHETAIROS: *[turning and chasing the Commissioner off stage]*
And I'll throw out those voting urns of yours!

STATUTE SELLER *[reappearing]*
Have you any memory of those evenings
when you used to shit on public pillars
where our laws are carved?

[The Statute Seller turns his back on Pisthetairos, lifts up his tunic, and farts at him]

PISTHETAIROS *[reacting to the smell]*
Oh god! Someone grab him.

[The slaves try to catch the Statute Seller but he runs off. Pisthetairos calls after him]

Not going to stick around?
[to slaves] Let's get out of here—and fast. Go inside.
We'll sacrifice the goat to the gods in there.

[Pisthetairos and the slaves to inside the house]

CHORUS
All mortal men commencing on this day
at every shrine will sacrifice to me,
from now on offering me the prayers they say,   [1060]
for I control them all and everything I see.
I watch the entire world, and I protect
the growing crops, for I have power to kill
the progeny of all the world's insects,
whose all-devouring jaws would eat their fill
of what bursts out from seeds on ground below,
or fruit above for those who lodge in trees.
I kill the ones who, as the greatest foe,
in sweet-smelling gardens cause great injuries
All living beasts that bite and crawl
are killed—my wings destroy them all.   [1070]

— τῇδε μέντοι θἠμέρᾳ μάλιστ' ἐπαναγορεύεται,

ἢν ἀποκτείνῃ τις ὑμῶν Διαγόραν τὸν Μήλιον,

λαμβάνειν τάλαντον, ἤν τε τῶν τυράννων τίς τινα

τῶν τεθνηκότων ἀποκτείνῃ, τάλαντον λαμβάνειν. 1075

βουλόμεσθ' οὖν νυν ἀνειπεῖν ταὐτὰ χἠμεῖς ἐνθάδε.

ἢν ἀποκτείνῃ τις ὑμῶν Φιλοκράτη τὸν Στρούθιον,

λήψεται τάλαντον, ἢν δὲ ζῶντά γ' ἀγάγῃ, τέτταρα,

ὅτι συνείρων τοὺς σπίνους πωλεῖ καθ' ἑπτὰ τοὐβολοῦ,

εἶτα φυσῶν τὰς κίχλας δείκνυσι καὶ λυμαίνεται, 1080

τοῖς τε κοψίχοισιν ἐς τὰς ῥῖνας ἐγχεῖ τὰ πτερά,

τὰς περιστεράς θ' ὁμοίως ξυλλαβὼν εἴρξας ἔχει,

κἀπαναγκάζει παλεύειν δεδεμένας ἐν δικτύῳ.

ταῦτα βουλόμεσθ' ἀνειπεῖν· κεἴ τις ὄρνιθας τρέφει

εἰργμένους ὑμῶν ἐν αὐλῇ, φράζομεν μεθιέναι. 1085

ἢν δὲ μὴ πίθησθε, συλληφθέντες ὑπὸ τῶν ὀρνέων

αὖθις ὑμεῖς αὖ παρ' ἡμῖν δεδεμένοι παλεύσετε.

— εὔδαιμον φῦλον πτηνῶν

οἰωνῶν, οἳ χειμῶνος μὲν

χλαίνας οὐκ ἀμπισχνοῦνται· 1090

οὐδ' αὖ θερμὴ πνίγους ἡμᾶς

ἀκτὶς τηλαυγὴς θάλπει·

ἀλλ' ἀνθηρῶν λειμώνων

φύλλων τ' ἐν κόλποις ναίω,

ἡνίκ' ἂν ὁ θεσπέσιος ὀξὺ μέλος ἀχέτας 1095

θάλπεσι μεσημβρινοῖς ἡλιομανὴς βοᾷ.

χειμάζω δ' ἐν κοίλοις ἄντροις

νύμφαοις οὐρείαις ξυμπαίζων·

CHORUS LEADER

This public notice has been proclaimed today:
the man who kills Diagoras the Melian
will receive one talent—and if one of you
assassinates some tyrant long since dead and gone,
he, too, will get one talent. So now, the birds, as well,
wish to make the same announcement here. Anyone
who kills Philocrates the Sparrowman will get
one talent—and if he brings him in alive,
he'll get four.[65] That man strings finches up together,
then sells 'em—a single obol gets you seven.
He injures thrushes by inflating them with air   [1080]
then puts them on display. And he stuff feathers
up the blackbird's nose. He captures pigeons, too,
keeps them locked up, and forces them to work for him,
tied up as decoy birds, underneath his nets.
We wish to make this known to you. If anyone
is keeping birds in cages in your courtyards,
we tell you, "Let them go." If you don't obey,
you, in your turn, will be arrested by the birds,
tied up and forced to work as decoys where we live.

CHORUS

    O happy tribes
    of feathered birds—
    we never need
    a winter cloak.   [1090]
    In summer days
    the sun's far rays
    don't injure us.
    I live at ease
    among the leaves
    in flowery fields.
    In love with sun
    cicadas sing
    through noonday heat
    their sharp-toned song
    divinely sweet.
    In winter caves
    and hollow spots
    I play all day
    with mountain nymphs.

Aristophanes

ἠρινά τε βοσκόμεθα παρθένια
λευκότροφα μύρτα Χαρίτων τε κηπεύματα.   1100

— τοῖς κριταῖς εἰπεῖν τι βουλόμεσθα τῆς νίκης πέρι,
ὅσ᾽ ἀγάθ᾽, ἢν κρίνωσιν ἡμᾶς, πᾶσιν αὐτοῖς δώσομεν,
ὥστε κρείττω δῶρα πολλῷ τῶν Ἀλεξάνδρου λαβεῖν.
πρῶτα μὲν γὰρ οὗ μάλιστα πᾶς κριτὴς ἐφίεται,   1105
γλαῦκες ὑμᾶς οὔποτ᾽ ἐπιλείψουσι Λαυρειωτικαί·
ἀλλ᾽ ἐνοικήσουσιν ἔνδον, ἔν τε τοῖς βαλλαντίοις
ἐννεοττεύσουσι κἀκλέψουσι μικρὰ κέρματα.
εἶτα πρὸς τούτοισιν ὥσπερ ἐν ἱεροῖς οἰκήσετε·
τὰς γὰρ ὑμῶν οἰκίας ἐρέψομεν πρὸς αἰετόν·   1110
κἂν λαχόντες ἀρχίδιον εἶθ᾽ ἁρπάσαι βούλησθέ τι,
ὀξὺν ἱερακίσκον ἐς τὰς χεῖρας ὑμῖν δώσομεν.
ἢν δέ που δειπνῆτε, πρηγορεῶνας ὑμῖν πέμψομεν.
ἢν δὲ μὴ κρίνητε, χαλκεύεσθε μηνίσκους φορεῖν
ὥσπερ ἀνδριάντες· ὡς ὑμῶν ὃς ἂν μὴ μῆν᾽ ἔχῃ,   1115
ὅταν ἔχητε χλανίδα λευκήν, τότε μάλισθ᾽ οὕτω δίκην
δώσεθ᾽ ἡμῖν, πᾶσι τοῖς ὄρνισι κατατιλώμενοι.

ΠΙΣΘΕΤΑΙΡΟΣ

τὰ μὲν ἱέρ᾽ ἡμῖν ἐστιν ὤρνιθες καλά·
ἀλλ᾽ ὡς ἀπὸ τοῦ τείχους πάρεστιν ἄγγελος
οὐδείς, ὅτου πευσόμεθα τἀκεῖ πράγματα.   1120
ἀλλ᾽ οὑτοσὶ τρέχει τις Ἀλφειὸν πνέων.

ΑΓΓΕΛΟΣ Α

ποῦ ποῦ ᾽στι, ποῦ ποῦ ποῦ ᾽στι, ποῦ ποῦ ποῦ ᾽στι ποῦ,
ποῦ Πισθέταιρός ἐστιν ἄρχων;

124

In spring we eat
white myrtle buds,
our virgin treat,
in garden places
of the Graces.   [1100]

CHORUS LEADER
We want to speak to all the judges here
about our victory—the splendid things
we'll give them if their verdict goes our way—
how they'll get much lovelier gifts than those
which Alexander got.[66] And first of all,
what every judge is really keen to have,
some owls of Laureium who'll never leave.[67]
They'll nest inside your homes, hatch in your purse,
and always breed small silver change. And then,
as well as this, you'll live in temple-homes.
The birds will make your roof tops eagle-style,   [1110]
with pediments.[68] If you hold some office,
a minor post, and wish to get rich quick,
we'll set a sharp-beaked falcon in your hands.
And if you need to eat, then we'll dispatch
a bird's crop, where it keep its stored-up food.
If you don't vote for us, you should prepare
some little metal plates to guard your head.
You'll need to wear them, just like statues do.
For those of you without that head plate on,
when you dress up in fine white brand-new clothes,
the birds will crap on as a punishment.

[Enter Pisthetairos from the house]

PISTHETAIROS
You birds, we've made a splendid sacrifice.
But why is there still no messenger
arriving from the walls to bring us news   [1120]
of what's going on up there? Ah, here comes one,
panting as if he'd run across that stream
at Elis where Olympian athletes race.

[Enter First Messenger, out of breath]

FIRST MESSENGER *[he doubles up and can hardly speak]*
Where is . . . Where is he . . . where . . . where is . . .
where . . . where . . . where . . . our governor Pisthetairos?

ΠΙΣΘΕΤΑΙΡΟΣ

οὑτοσί.

ἌΓΓΕΛΟΣ Α

ἐξῳκοδόμηταί σοι τὸ τεῖχος.

ΠΙΣΘΕΤΑΙΡΟΣ

εὖ λέγεις.

ἌΓΓΕΛΟΣ Α

κάλλιστον ἔργον καὶ μεγαλοπρεπέστατον·   1125
ὥστ᾽ ἂν ἐπάνω μὲν Προξενίδης ὁ Κομπασεὺς
καὶ Θεογένης ἐναντίω δύ᾽ ἅρματε,
ἵππων ὑπόντων μέγεθος ὅσον ὁ δούριος,
ὑπὸ τοῦ πλάτους ἂν παρελασαίτην.

ΠΙΣΘΕΤΑΙΡΟΣ

Ἡράκλεις.

ἌΓΓΕΛΟΣ Α

τὸ δὲ μῆκός ἐστι, καὶ γὰρ ἐμέτρησ᾽ αὔτ᾽ ἐγώ,   1130
ἑκατοντορόγυιον.

ΠΙΣΘΕΤΑΙΡΟΣ

ὦ Πόσειδον τοῦ μάκρους.
τίνες ᾠκοδόμησαν αὐτὸ τηλικουτονί;

ἌΓΓΕΛΟΣ Α

ὄρνιθες, οὐδεὶς ἄλλος, οὐκ Αἰγύπτιος
πλινθοφόρος, οὐ λιθουργός, οὐ τέκτων παρῆν,
ἀλλ᾽ αὐτόχειρες, ὥστε θαυμάζειν ἐμέ.   1135
ἐκ μέν γε Λιβύης ἧκον ὡς τρισμύριαι
γέρανοι θεμελίους καταπεπωκυῖαι λίθους.
τούτους δ᾽ ἐτύκιζον αἱ κρέκες τοῖς ῥύγχεσιν.
ἕτεροι δ᾽ ἐπλινθοφόρουν πελαργοὶ μύριοι·
ὕδωρ δ᾽ ἐφόρουν κάτωθεν ἐς τὸν ἀέρα   1140
οἱ χαραδριοὶ καὶ τἆλλα ποτόμι᾽ ὄρνεα.

ΠΙΣΘΕΤΑΙΡΟΣ

ἐπηλοφόρουν δ᾽ αὐτοῖσι τίνες;

PISTHETAIROS
    I'm here.

FIRST MESSENGER
    The building of your wall . . . it's done.

PISTHETAIROS
    That's great news.

FIRST MESSENGER
              The result — the best there is . . .
    the most magnificent . . . so wide across . . .
    that Proxenides of Braggadocio
    and Theogenes could drive two chariots
    in opposite directions past each other
    along the top, with giant horses yoked,
    bigger than that wooden horse at Troy.

PISTHETAIROS *[genuinely surprised]*
    By Hercules!

FIRST MESSENGER
              I measured it myself —   [1130]
    its height — around six hundred feet.

PISTHETAIROS
                              Wow!
    By Poseidon, that's some height! Who built the wall
    as high as that?

FIRST MESSENGER
              The birds — nobody else.
    No Egyptian bore the bricks — no mason,
    no carpenter was there. They worked by hand —
    I was amazed. Thirty thousand cranes flew in
    from Lybia — they brought foundation stones
    they'd swallowed down. The corn crakes chipped away
    to form the proper shapes. Ten thousand storks
    brought bricks. Lapwings and other river birds
    fetched water up into the air from down below.   [1140]

PISTHETAIROS
    Who hauled the mortar up there for them?

ἈΓΓΕΛΟΣ Α

λεκάναισι.

ἐρωδιοὶ

ΠΙΣΘΕΤΑΙΡΟΣ

τὸν δὲ πηλὸν ἐνεβάλλοντο πῶς;

ἈΓΓΕΛΟΣ Α

τοῦτ' ὦγάθ' ἐξηύρητο καὶ σοφώτατα·
οἱ χῆνες ὑποτύπτοντες ὥσπερ ταῖς ἅμαις   1145
ἐς τὰς λεκάνας ἐνέβαλλον αὐτοῖς τοῖν ποδοῖν.

ΠΙΣΘΕΤΑΙΡΟΣ

τί δῆτα πόδες ἂν οὐκ ἂν ἐργασαίατο;

ἈΓΓΕΛΟΣ Α

καὶ νὴ Δί' αἱ νῆτταί γε περιεζωσμέναι
ἐπλινθοφόρουν· ἄνω δὲ τὸν ὑπαγωγέα
ἐπέτοντ' ἔχουσαι κατόπιν †ὥσπερ παιδία   1150
τὸν πηλὸν ἐν τοῖς στόμασιν† αἱ χελιδόνες.

ΠΙΣΘΕΤΑΙΡΟΣ

τί δῆτα μισθωτοὺς ἂν ἔτι μισθοῖτό τις;
φέρ' ἴδω, τί δαί; τὰ ξύλινα τοῦ τείχους τίνες
ἀπηργάσαντ';

ἈΓΓΕΛΟΣ Α

ὄρνιθες ἦσαν τέκτονες
σοφώτατοι πελεκᾶντες, οἳ τοῖς ῥύγχεσιν   1155
ἀπεπελέκησαν τὰς πύλας· ἦν δ' ὁ κτύπος
αὐτῶν πελεκώντων ὥσπερ ἐν ναυπηγίῳ.
καὶ νῦν ἅπαντ' ἐκεῖνα πεπύλωται πύλαις
καὶ βεβαλάνωται καὶ φυλάττεται κύκλῳ,
ἐφοδεύεται, κωδωνοφορεῖται, πανταχῇ,   1160
φυλακαὶ καθεστήκασι καὶ φρυκτωρίαι
ἐν τοῖσι πύργοις. ἀλλ' ἐγὼ μὲν ἀποτρέχων
ἀπονίψομαι· σὺ δ' αὐτὸς ἤδη τἆλλα δρᾶ.

ΧΟΡΟΣ

οὗτος τί ποιεῖς; ἆρα θαυμάζεις ὅτι
οὕτω τὸ τεῖχος ἐκτετείχισται ταχύ;   1165

128

FIRST MESSENGER

Herons—
they carried hods.

PISTHETAIROS

How'd they load those hods?

FIRST MESSENGER

My dear man, that was the cleverest thing of all.
Geese shoved their feet into the muck and slid them,
just like shovels, then flicked it in the hods.

PISTHETAIROS

Is there anything we can't do with our feet?

FIRST MESSENGER

Then, by god, the ducks, with slings attached
around their waists, set up the bricks. Behind them
flew the swallows, like young apprentice boys,   [1150]
with trowels—they carried mortar in their mouths.

PISTHETAIROS

Why should we hire wage labour any more?
Go on—who finished off the woodwork on the wall?

FIRST MESSENGER

The most skilled craftsmen-birds of all of 'em—
woodpeckers. They pecked away to make the gates—
the noise those peckers made—an arsenal!
Now the whole thing has gates. They're bolted shut
and guarded on all sides. Sentries make rounds,
patrolling with their bells, and everywhere   [1160]
troops are in position, with signal fires
on every tower. But I must go now—
I need to wash. You'll have to do the rest.

[Exit First Messenger]

CHORUS LEADER

What's up with you? Aren't you astonished
to hear the wall's been finished up so fast?

ΠΙΣΘΕΤΑΙΡΟΣ
νὴ τοὺς θεοὺς ἔγωγε· καὶ γὰρ ἄξιον·
ἴσα γὰρ ἀληθῶς φαίνεταί μοι ψεύδεσιν.
ἀλλ' ὅδε φύλαξ γὰρ τῶν ἐκεῖθεν ἄγγελος
ἐσθεῖ πρὸς ἡμᾶς δεῦρο πυρρίχην βλέπων.

ΑΓΓΕΛΟΣ Β
ἰοὺ ἰού, ἰοὺ ἰού, ἰοὺ ἰού.   1170

ΠΙΣΘΕΤΑΙΡΟΣ
τί τὸ πρᾶγμα τουτί;

ΑΓΓΕΛΟΣ Β
                        δεινότατα πεπόνθαμεν.
τῶν γὰρ θεῶν τις ἄρτι τῶν παρὰ τοῦ Διὸς
διὰ τῶν πυλῶν εἰσέπτετ' ἐς τὸν ἀέρα,
λαθὼν κολοιοὺς φύλακας ἡμεροσκόπους.

ΠΙΣΘΕΤΑΙΡΟΣ
ὦ δεινὸν ἔργον καὶ σχέτλιον εἰργασμένος.   1175
τίς τῶν θεῶν;

ΑΓΓΕΛΟΣ Β
                    οὐκ ἴσμεν· ὅτι δ' εἶχε πτερά,
τοῦτ' ἴσμεν.

ΠΙΣΘΕΤΑΙΡΟΣ
                    οὔκουν δῆτα περιπόλους ἐχρῆν
πέμψαι κατ' αὐτὸν εὐθύς;

ΑΓΓΕΛΟΣ Β
                            ἀλλ' ἐπέμψαμεν
τρισμυρίους ἱέρακας ἱπποτοξότας,
χωρεῖ δὲ πᾶς τις ὄνυχας ἠγκυλωμένος,   1180
κερχνῇς τριόρχης γὺψ κύμινδις αἰετός·
ῥύμῃ τε καὶ πτεροῖσι καὶ ῥοιζήμασιν
αἰθὴρ δονεῖται τοῦ θεοῦ ζητουμένου·
κἄστ' οὐ μακρὰν ἄπωθεν, ἀλλ' ἐνταῦθά που
ἤδη 'στίν.   1185

PISTHETAIROS

Yes, by gods, I am. It is amazing!
To me it sounds just like some made-up lie.
But here comes a guard from there—he'll bring news
to us down here of what's going on up top.
He face looks like a dancing warrior's.

[Enter the Second Messenger in a great panic and out of breath]

SECOND MESSENGER

Hey . . . hey . . . Help . . . hey you . . . help!   [1170]

PISTHETAIROS

What's going on?

SECOND MESSENGER

        We suffered something really bad . . .
one of the gods from Zeus has just got through,
flown past the gates into the air, slipping by
the jackdaw sentinels on daytime watch.

PISTHETAIROS

That's bad! A bold and dangerous action.
Which god was it?

SECOND MESSENGER

        We're not sure. He had wings—
we do know that.

PISTHETAIROS

        You should have sent patrols
of frontier guards out after him without delay.

SECOND MESSENGER

We did dispatch the mounted archers—
thirty thousand falcons, all moving out   [1180]
with talons curved and ready—kestrels, buzzards,
vultures, eagles, owls—the air vibrating
with the beat and rustle of their wings,
as they search out that god. He's not far off—
in fact, he's here somewhere already.

[Exit Second Messenger]

ΠΙΣΘΕΤΑΙΡΟΣ

οὔκουν σφενδόνας δεῖ λαμβάνειν
καὶ τόξα; χώρει δεῦρο πᾶς ὑπηρέτης·
τόξευε παῖ, σφενδόνην τίς μοι δότω.

ΧΟΡΟΣ

πόλεμος αἴρεται, πόλεμος οὐ φατὸς
πρὸς ἐμὲ καὶ θεούς. ἀλλὰ φύλαττε πᾶς   1190
ἀέρα περινέφελον, ὃν ἔρεβος ἐτέκετο,
μή σε λάθῃ θεῶν τις ταύτῃ περῶν·   1195
.... ἄθρει δὲ πᾶς κύκλῳ σκοπῶν,
ὡς ἐγγὺς ἤδη δαίμονος πεδαρσίου
δίνης πτερωτὸς φθόγγος ἐξακούεται.

ΠΙΣΘΕΤΑΙΡΟΣ

αὕτη σύ, ποῖ ποῖ ποῖ πέτει; μέν᾽ ἥσυχος,
ἔχ᾽ ἀτρέμας· αὐτοῦ στῆθ᾽· ἐπίσχες τοῦ δρόμου.   1200
τίς εἶ; ποδαπή; λέγειν ἐχρῆν ὁπόθεν ποτ᾽ εἶ.

ΙΡΙΣ

παρὰ τῶν θεῶν ἔγωγε τῶν Ὀλυμπίων.

ΠΙΣΘΕΤΑΙΡΟΣ

ὄνομα δέ σο. τί ἐστι; πλοῖον ἢ κυνῆ;

ΙΡΙΣ

Ἶρις ταχεῖα.

ΠΙΣΘΕΤΑΙΡΟΣ

        Πάραλος ἢ Σαλαμινία;

ΙΡΙΣ

τί δὲ τοῦτο;   1205

ΠΙΣΘΕΤΑΙΡΟΣ

        ταυτηνί τις οὐ συλλήψεται
ἀναπτόμενος τρίορχος;

ΙΡΙΣ

           ἐμὲ συλλήψεται;
τί ποτ᾽ ἐστὶ τουτὶ τὸ κακόν;

PISTHETAIROS
> We'll have to get our sling-shots out — and bows.
> All you orderlies come here! Fire away!
> Strike out! Someone fetch a sling for me!

[Xanthias and Manodorus enter with slings and bows. The group huddles together with weapons ready]

CHORUS *[in grand epic style]*
> And now the combat starts, a strife beyond all words,
> me and the gods at war. Let everyone beware,   [1190]
> protect the cloud-enclosing air, which Erebus
> gave birth to long ago. Make sure no god slips through
> without our catching sight of him. Maintain your watch
> on every side — already I can hear close by
> the sound of beating wings from some god in the sky.

[Enter Iris, in long billowing dress and with a pair of wings. She descends from above, suspended by a cable and hovering in mid-air flapping her wings]

PISTHETAIROS
> Hey, you — just where do you think you're flying?
> Keep still. Stay where you are. Don't move. Stop running.   [1200]
> Who are you? Where you from? You've got to tell me.
> Where'd you come from?

IRIS
> I'm from the Olympian gods.

PISTHETAIROS
> You got a name? You look like a ship up there —
> the Salaminia or the Paralos.[69]

IRIS
> I'm fast Iris.

PISTHETAIROS
> Fast as in a boat or fast as in a bitch?

IRIS
> What is all this?

PISTHETAIROS
> Is there a buzzard here
> who'll fly up there to arrest this woman?

IRIS
> Arrest me? Why are you saying such rubbish?

ΠΙΣΘΕΤΑΙΡΟΣ

οἰμώξει μακρά.

ΙΡΙΣ

ἄτοπόν γε τουτὶ πρᾶγμα.

ΠΙΣΘΕΤΑΙΡΟΣ

κατὰ ποίας πύλας

εἰσῆλθες ἐς τὸ τεῖχος ὦ μιαρωτάτη;

ΙΡΙΣ

οὐκ οἶδα μὰ Δί᾽ ἔγωγε κατὰ ποίας πύλας.   1210

ΠΙΣΘΕΤΑΙΡΟΣ

ἤκουσας αὐτῆς οἷον εἰρωνεύεται;

πρὸς τοὺς κολοιάρχας προσῆλθες; οὐ λέγεις;

σφραγῖδ᾽ ἔχεις παρὰ τῶν πελαργῶν;

ΙΡΙΣ

τί τὸ κακόν.

ΠΙΣΘΕΤΑΙΡΟΣ

οὐκ ἔλαβες;

ΙΡΙΣ

ὑγιαίνεις μέν;

ΠΙΣΘΕΤΑΙΡΟΣ

οὐδὲ σύμβολον

ἐπέβαλεν ὀρνίθαρχος οὐδείς σοι παρών;   1215

ΙΡΙΣ

μὰ Δί᾽ οὐκ ἔμοιγ᾽ ἐπέβαλεν οὐδεὶς ὦ μέλε.

ΠΙΣΘΕΤΑΙΡΟΣ

κἄπειτα δῆθ᾽ οὕτω σιωπῇ διαπέτει

διὰ τῆς πόλεως τῆς ἀλλοτρίας καὶ τοῦ χάους;

ΙΡΙΣ

ποίᾳ γὰρ ἄλλῃ χρὴ πέτεσθαι τοὺς θεούς;

ΠΙΣΘΕΤΑΙΡΟΣ

οὐκ οἶδα μὰ Δί᾽ ἔγωγε· τῇδε μὲν γὰρ οὔ.   1220

ἀδικεῖς δὲ καὶ νῦν. ἀρά γ᾽ οἶσθα τοῦθ᾽ ὅτι

134

PISTHETAIROS *[making at attempt to hit Iris by swinging his sling]*
You're going to be very sorry about this.

IRIS

This whole affair is most unusual.

PISTHETAIROS

Listen, you silly old fool, what gates
did you pass through to get by the wall?

IRIS

What gates?
By god, I don't have the least idea. [1210]

PISTHETAIROS

Listen to her—how she feigns ignorance!
Did you go past the jackdaw generals?
You won't answer that? Well then, where's your pass,
the one the storks give out?

IRIS

What's wrong with you?

PISTHETAIROS

You don't have one, do you?

IRIS

Have you lost your wits?

PISTHETAIROS

Didn't some captain of the birds up there
stick a pass on you?

IRIS

By god no, no one up there
made a pass or shoved his stick at me, you wretch.

PISTHETAIROS

So you just fly in here, without a word,
going through empty space and through a city
which don't belong to you?

IRIS

What other route
are gods supposed to fly?

PISTHETAIROS

I've no idea.
But, by god, not this way. It's not legal. [1220]
Right now you're in breach of law. Do you know,

δικαιότατ᾽ ἂν ληφθεῖσα πασῶν Ἰρίδων
ἀπέθανες, εἰ τῆς ἀξίας ἐτύγχανες;

ΙΡΙΣ

                       ἀλλ᾽ ἀθάνατός εἰμ᾽.

ΠΙΣΘΕΤΑΙΡΟΣ

ἀλλ᾽ ὅμως ἂν ἀπέθανες.
δεινότατα γάρ τοι πεισόμεσθ᾽, ἐμοὶ δοκεῖ,   1225
εἰ τῶν μὲν ἄλλων ἄρχομεν, ὑμεῖς δ᾽ οἱ θεοὶ
ἀκολαστανεῖτε, κοὐδέπω γνώσεσθ᾽ ὅτι
ἀκροατέον ὑμῖν ἐν μέρει τῶν κρειττόνων.
φράσον δέ τοί μοι τὼ πτέρυγε ποῖ ναυστολεῖς;

ΙΡΙΣ

ἐγώ; πρὸς ἀνθρώπους πέτομαι παρὰ τοῦ πατρὸς   1230
φράσουσα θύειν τοῖς Ὀλυμπίοις θεοῖς
μηλοσφαγεῖν τε βουθύτοις ἐπ᾽ ἐσχάραις
κνισᾶν τ᾽ ἀγυιάς.

ΠΙΣΘΕΤΑΙΡΟΣ

            τί σὺ λέγεις; ποίοις θεοῖς;

ΙΡΙΣ

ποίοισιν; ἡμῖν τοῖς ἐν οὐρανῷ θεοῖς.

ΠΙΣΘΕΤΑΙΡΟΣ

θεοὶ γὰρ ὑμεῖς;   1235

ΙΡΙΣ

             τίς γάρ ἐστ᾽ ἄλλος θεός;

ΠΙΣΘΕΤΑΙΡΟΣ

ὄρνιθες ἀνθρώποισι νῦν εἰσιν θεοί,
οἷς θυτέον αὐτούς, ἀλλὰ μὰ Δί᾽ οὐ τῷ Διί.

ΙΡΙΣ

ὦ μῶρε μῶρε μὴ θεῶν κίνει φρένας
δεινάς, ὅπως μή σου γένος πανώλεθρον
Διὸς μακέλλῃ πᾶν ἀναστρέψῃ Δίκη,   1240
λιγνὺς δὲ σῶμα καὶ δόμων περιπτυχὰς
καταιθαλώσῃ σου Λικυμνίαις βολαῖς.

of all the Irises there are around,
if you got what you most deserve, you'd be
the one most justly seized and sent to die.

IRIS

But I'm immortal.

PISTHETAIROS

In spite of that,
you would have died. For it's obvious to me
that we'd be suffering the greatest injury,
if, while we rule all other things, you gods
do just what you like and won't recognize
how you must, in your turn, attend upon
those more powerful than you. So tell me,
where are you sailing on those wings of yours?

IRIS

Me? I'm flying to men from father Zeus,   [1230]
instructing them to sacrifice some sheep
to the Olympian gods on sacred hearths —
and fill their streets with smells of offerings.

PISTHETAIROS

Who are you talking about? Which gods?

IRIS

Which gods? Why us of course — the gods in heaven.

PISTHETAIROS

And you're the gods?

IRIS

Are there any other deities?

PISTHETAIROS

The birds are now men's gods — and to the birds
men must now sacrifice and not, by god, to Zeus.

IRIS [*in the grand tragic style*]
Thou fool, thou fool, stir not the awesome minds of gods,
lest Justice with the mighty mattock of great Zeus   [1240]
destroy your race completely — and smoke-filled flames
from Licymnian lightning bolts burn into ash
your body and your home . . .

137

ΠΙΣΘΕΤΑΙΡΟΣ
ἄκουσον αὕτη· παῦε τῶν παφλασμάτων·
ἔχ᾽ ἀτρέμα. φέρ᾽ ἴδω, πότερα Λυδὸν ἢ Φρύγα
ταυτὶ λέγουσα μορμολύττεσθαι δοκεῖς;   1245
ἆρ᾽ οἶσθ᾽ ὅτι Ζεὺς εἴ με λυπήσει πέρα,
μέλαθρα μὲν αὐτοῦ καὶ δόμους Ἀμφίονος
καταιθαλώσω πυρφόροισιν αἰετοῖς;
πέμψω δὲ πορφυρίωνας ἐς τὸν οὐρανὸν
ὄρνις ἐπ᾽ αὐτὸν παρδαλᾶς ἐνημμένους   1250
πλεῖν ἑξακοσίους τὸν ἀριθμόν. καὶ δή ποτε
εἷς Πορφυρίων αὐτῷ παρέσχε πράγματα.
σὺ δ᾽ εἴ με λυπήσεις τι, τῆς διακόνου
πρώτης ἀνατείνας τὼ σκέλει διαμηριῶ
τὴν Ἶριν αὐτήν, ὥστε θαυμάζειν ὅπως   1255
οὕτω γέρων ὢν στύομαι τριέμβολον.

ΙΡΙΣ
διαρραγείης ὦ μέλ᾽ αὐτοῖς ῥήμασιν.

ΠΙΣΘΕΤΑΙΡΟΣ
οὐκ ἀποσοβήσεις; οὐ ταχέως; εὐρὰξ πατάξ.

ΙΡΙΣ
ἦ μήν σε παύσει τῆς ὕβρεως οὑμὸς πατήρ.

ΠΙΣΘΕΤΑΙΡΟΣ
οἴμοι τάλας. οὔκουν ἑτέρωσε πετομένη   1260
καταιθαλώσεις τῶν νεωτέρων τινά;

ΧΟΡΟΣ
ἀποκεκλήκαμεν διογενεῖς θεοὺς
μηκέτι τὴν ἐμὴν διαπερᾶν πόλιν,
μηδέ γέ τιν᾽ ἱερόθυτον ἀνὰ δάπεδον ἔτι   1265
τῇδε βροτῶν θεοῖσι πέμπειν καπνόν.

ΠΙΣΘΕΤΑΙΡΟΣ
δεινόν γε τὸν κήρυκα τὸν παρὰ τοὺς βροτοὺς
οἰχόμενον, εἰ μηδέποτε νοστήσει πάλιν.   1270

PISTHETAIROS *[interrupting]*
>Listen, woman—stop your spluttering.
>Just keep still. Do you think you're scaring off
>some Lydian or Phrygian with such threats?
>You should know this—if Zeus keeps on annoying me,
>I'll burn his home and halls of Amphion,
>reduce them all to ash with fire eagles.
>I'll send more than six hundred birds—porphyrions
>all dressed in leopard skins, up there to heaven,   [1250]
>to war on him. Once a single porphyrion
>caused him distress enough.[70] And as for you,
>if you keep trying to piss me off, well then,
>I'll deal with Zeus' servant Iris first—
>I'll fuck your knickers off—you'd be surprised
>how hard an old man's prick like mine can be—
>it's strong enough to ram your hull three times.

IRIS
>Blast you, you wretch, and your obscenities!

PISTHETAIROS
>Go way! Get a move on! Shoo!

[Iris begins to move up and away]

IRIS
>   My father
>won't stand for insolence like this—he'll stop you!

PISTHETAIROS
>Just go away, you silly fool! Fly off   [1210]
>and burn someone to ashes somewhere else.

[Exit Iris]

CHORUS
>On Zeus' family of gods we've shut our door—
>they'll not be passing through my city any more.
>Nor will men down below in future time invoke
>the gods by sending them their sacrificial smoke.

PISTHETAIROS
>Something's wrong. That messenger we sent,
>the one that went to human beings, what if
>he never gets back here again?   [1270]

ΚΗΡΥΞ Α

ὦ Πισθέταιρ᾽ ὦ μακάρι᾽ ὦ σοφώτατε,
ὦ κλεινότατ᾽ ὦ σοφώτατ᾽ ὦ γλαφυρώτατε,
ὦ τρισμακάρι᾽ ὦ κατακέλευσον.

ΠΙΣΘΕΤΑΙΡΟΣ

τί σὺ λέγεις;

ΚΗΡΥΞ Α

στεφάνῳ σε χρυσῷ τῷδε σοφίας οὕνεκα
στεφανοῦσι καὶ τιμῶσιν οἱ πάντες λεῴ.   1275

ΠΙΣΘΕΤΑΙΡΟΣ

δέχομαι. τί δ᾽ οὕτως οἱ λεῴ τιμῶσί με;

ΚΗΡΥΞ Α

ὦ κλεινοτάτην αἰθέριον οἰκίσας πόλιν,
οὐκ οἶσθ᾽ ὅσην τιμὴν παρ᾽ ἀνθρώποις φέρει,
ὅσους τ᾽ ἐραστὰς τῆσδε τῆς χώρας ἔχεις.
πρὶν μὲν γὰρ οἰκίσαι σε τήνδε τὴν πόλιν,   1280
ἐλακωνομάνουν ἅπαντες ἄνθρωποι τότε,
ἐκόμων ἐπείνων ἐρρύπων ἐσωκράτουν
σκυτάλι᾽ ἐφόρουν, νυνὶ δ᾽ ὑποστρέψαντες αὖ
ὀρνιθομανοῦσι, πάντα δ᾽ ὑπὸ τῆς ἡδονῆς
ποιοῦσιν ἅπερ ὄρνιθες ἐκμιμούμενοι·   1285
πρῶτον μὲν εὐθὺς πάντες ἐξ εὐνῆς ἅμα
ἐπέτονθ᾽ ἕωθεν ὥσπερ ἡμεῖς ἐπὶ νομόν·
κἄπειτ᾽ ἂν ἅμα κατῆραν ἐς τὰ βιβλία·
εἶτ᾽ ἀπενέμοντ᾽ ἐνταῦθα τὰ ψηφίσματα.
ὠρνιθομάνουν δ᾽ οὕτω περιφανῶς ὥστε καὶ   1290
πολλοῖσιν ὀρνίθων ὀνόματ᾽ ἦν κείμενα.
πέρδιξ μὲν εἷς κάπηλος ὠνομάζετο
χωλός, Μενίππῳ δ᾽ ἦν χελιδὼν τοὔνομα,
Ὀπουντίῳ δ᾽ ὀφθαλμὸν οὐκ ἔχων κόραξ,
κορυδὸς Φιλοκλέει, χηναλώπηξ Θεογένει,   1295
ἶβις Λυκούργῳ, Χαιρεφῶντι νυκτερίς,
Συρακοσίῳ δὲ κίττα· Μειδίας δ᾽ ἐκεῖ

[Enter First Herald, a bird, carrying a golden crown]

FIRST HERALD

> O Pisthetairos, you blessed one,
> wisest and most celebrated of all men . . .
> the cleverest and happiest . . . trebly blest . . .
> *[He's run out of adjectives]* . . . Speak something to me . . .

PISTHETAIROS

> What are you saying?

FIRST HERALD *[offering Pisthetairos the golden crown]*
> All people, in honour of your wisdom,
> crown you with this golden diadem.

PISTHETAIROS *[putting on the crown]*

> I accept.
> But why do people honour me so much?

FIRST HERALD

> O you founder of this most famous town,
> this city in the sky, do you not know
> how much respect you have among all men,
> how many men there are who love this place?
> Before you built your city in the air,   [1280]
> all men were mad for Sparta — with long hair,
> they went around half starved and never washed,
> like Socrates — and carrying knobbed sticks.
> But now they've all completely changed — these days
> they're crazy for the birds. For sheer delight
> they imitate the birds in everything.
> Early in the day when they've just got up,
> like us, they all flock to feed together,
> but on their laws, browsing legal leaflets,
> nibbling their fill of all decrees. So mad
> have they become for birds that many men   [1290]
> have had the names of birds assigned to them.
> One lame tradesman now is called the Partridge.
> And Melanippus' name is changed to Swallow,[71]
> Opuntius the Raven with One Eye.
> Philocles becomes the Lark, and Sheldrake
> is now Teagenes' name. Lycurgus
> has become the Ibis, Chaerephon the Bat,
> Syracosius the Jay, and Meidias

ὄρτυξ ἐκαλεῖτο· καὶ γὰρ ἥκειν ὄρτυγι
ὑπὸ στυφοκόπου τὴν κεφαλὴν πεπληγμένῳ.
ᾖδον δ᾽ ὑπὸ φιλορνιθίας πάντες μέλη,   1300
ὅπου χελιδὼν ἦν τις ἐμπεποιημένη
ἢ πηνέλοψ ἢ χήν τις ἢ περιστερὰ
ἢ πτέρυγες, ἢ πτεροῦ τι καὶ σμικρὸν προσῆν.
τοιαῦτα μὲν τἀκεῖθεν. ἓν δέ σοι λέγω·
ἥξουσ᾽ ἐκεῖθεν δεῦρο πλεῖν ἢ μύριοι   1305
πτερῶν δεόμενοι καὶ τρόπων γαμψωνύχων·
ὥστε πτερῶν σοι τοῖς ἐποίκοις δεῖ ποθέν.

ΠΙΣΘΕΤΑΙΡΟΣ
  οὐκ ἄρα μὰ Δί᾽ ἡμῖν ἔτ᾽ ἔργον ἑστάναι.
  ἀλλ᾽ ὡς τάχιστα σὺ μὲν ἰὼν τὰς ἀρρίχους
  καὶ τοὺς κοφίνους ἅπαντας ἐμπίμπλη πτερῶν·   1310
  Μανῆς δὲ φερέτω μοι θύραζε τὰ πτερά·
  ἐγὼ δ᾽ ἐκείνων τοὺς προσιόντας δέξομαι.

ΧΟΡΟΣ
  ταχὺ δὴ πολυάνορα τάνδε πόλιν
    καλεῖ τις ἀνθρώπων.

ΠΙΣΘΕΤΑΙΡΟΣ
      τύχη μόνον προσείη.   1315

ΧΟΡΟΣ
  κατέχουσι δ᾽ ἔρωτες ἐμᾶς πόλεως.

ΠΙΣΘΕΤΑΙΡΟΣ
      θᾶττον φέρειν κελεύω.

ΧΟΡΟΣ
    τί γὰρ οὐκ ἔνι ταύτῃ
      καλὸν ἀνδρὶ μετοικεῖν;
  Σοφία Πόθος Ἀμβροσία Χάριτες   1320
  τό τε τῆς ἀγανόφρονος Ἡσυχίας
    εὐήμερον πρόσωπον.

ΠΙΣΘΕΤΑΙΡΟΣ
  ὡς βλακικῶς διακονεῖς·
    οὐ θᾶττον ἐγκονήσεις;

is now named the Quail — he looks like one
right after the quail flicker's tapped its head.[72]
They're so in love with birds they all sing songs   [1300]
with lines about a swallow or a duck,
or goose, some kind of pigeon, or just wings,
even about some tiny bits of feather.
That what's going on down there. I tell you,
more than ten thousand men are coming here,
demanding wings and talons in their lives.
You've got to find a way to get some wings
for your new colonists and settlers.

[Exit First Herald]

PISTHETAIROS

All right, by god, this is no time for us
to just stand around. *[To a slave]* You, get inside there —
fill all the crates and baskets up with feathers.   [1310]
Get on with it as fast as possible.
Let Manes haul the wings out here to me.[73]
I'll welcome those who come from down below.

[Xanthias and Manodoros go inside the house and start bringing out baskets of feathers]

CHORUS

Our city soon will have a reputation
for a large and swelling population.

PISTHETAIROS

Just let our luck hold out!

CHORUS

Our city here inspires so much love . . .

PISTHETAIROS *[to Manodoros, who is bringing out a basket]*

I'm telling you you've got to bring it fast!

CHORUS

For what do we not have here up above
which any men require in their places?
Desire, Wisdom, and eternal Graces —
we've got them all and what is still the best —
the happy face of gentle peaceful Rest.

PISTHETAIROS *[to Manes who is taking his time bringing out more baskets]*

God, you're a lazy slave — move it! Faster!

ΧΟΡΟΣ

φερέτω κάλαθον ταχύ τις πτερύγων,　　　1325
σὺ δ' αὖθις ἐξόρμα—
τύπτων γε τοῦτον ὡδί.
πάνυ γὰρ βραδύς ἐστί τις ὥσπερ ὄνος.

ΠΙΣΘΕΤΑΙΡΟΣ

Μανῆς γάρ ἐστι δειλός.

ΧΟΡΟΣ

σὺ δὲ τὰ πτερὰ πρῶτον　　　1330
διάθες τάδε κόσμῳ,
τά τε μουσίχ' ὁμοῦ τά τε μαντικὰ καὶ
τὰ θαλάττι'. ἔπειτα δ' ὅπως φρονίμως
πρὸς ἄνδρ' ὁρῶν πτερώσεις.

ΠΙΣΘΕΤΑΙΡΟΣ

οὔ τοι μὰ τὰς κερχνῇδας ἔτι σοῦ σχήσομαι,　　　1335
οὕτως ὁρῶν σε δειλὸν ὄντα καὶ βραδύν.

ΠΑΤΡΑΛΟΙΑΣ

γενοίμαν αἰετὸς ὑψιπέτας,
ὡς ἀμποταθείην ὑπὲρ ἀτρυγέτου
γλαυκᾶς ἐπ' οἶδμα λίμνας.

ΠΙΣΘΕΤΑΙΡΟΣ

ἔοικεν οὐ ψευδαγγελήσειν ἄγγελος.　　　1340
ᾄδων γὰρ ὅδε τις αἰετοὺς προσέρχεται.

ΠΑΤΡΑΛΟΙΑΣ

αἰβοῖ·
οὐκ ἔστιν οὐδὲν τοῦ πέτεσθαι γλυκύτερον·
ὀρνιθομανῶ γὰρ καὶ πέτομαι καὶ βούλομαι
οἰκεῖν μεθ' ὑμῶν κἀπιθυμῶ τῶν νόμων.　　　1345

ΠΙΣΘΕΤΑΙΡΟΣ

ποίων νόμων; πολλοὶ γὰρ ὀρνίθων νόμοι.

CHORUS

> Let him bring the wings in baskets on the go —
> then once more run at him — give him a blow.
> The lad is like a donkey — he's that slow.

PISTHETAIROS *[frantically sorting feathers]*

> Yes, that Manes is a useless slave.

CHORUS

> Now first of all you need to sort   [1330]
> these wings all out for each cohort —
> musical wings and wings of seers,
> wings for the sea. You must be clear —
> you need to look at all such things
> when you give every man his wings.

[Manes comes out with a basket, again moving very slowly]

PISTHETAIROS *[going at Manes and grabbling him]*

> By the kestrels, I can't stop grabbing you —
> when I see how miserably slow you are.

[Manes twists loose and runs back into the house. A young man enters singing]

YOUNG MAN *[singing]*

> Oh, I wish I could an eagle be
> soaring high above the barren sea,
> the grey-blue ocean swell so free.

PISTHETAIROS

> It looks like our messenger told us the truth —
> here comes someone singing that eagle-song.

YOUNG MAN

> Damn it — there's nothing in the world as sweet
> as flying . . .

PISTHETAIROS

> You've come to get some wings from us, I guess.74

YOUNG MAN

> Yes, I'm in love with all your birdy ways —
> I want to live with you and fly. Besides,
> I think your laws are really keen.

PISTHETAIROS

> What laws? The birds have many laws.

ΠΑΤΡΑΛΟΙΑΣ
πάντων· μάλιστα δ' ὅτι καλὸν νομίζεται
τὸν πατέρα τοῖς ὄρνισιν ἄγχειν καὶ δάκνειν.

ΠΙΣΘΕΤΑΙΡΟΣ
καὶ νὴ Δί' ἀνδρεῖόν γε πάνυ νομίζομεν,
ὃς ἂν πεπλήγῃ τὸν πατέρα νεοττὸς ὤν.   1350

ΠΑΤΡΑΛΟΙΑΣ
διὰ ταῦτα μέντοι δεῦρ' ἀνοικισθεὶς ἐγὼ
ἄγχειν ἐπιθυμῶ τὸν πατέρα καὶ πάντ' ἔχειν.

ΠΙΣΘΕΤΑΙΡΟΣ
ἀλλ' ἔστιν ἡμῖν τοῖσιν ὄρνισιν νόμος
παλαιὸς ἐν ταῖς τῶν πελαργῶν κύρβεσιν·
ἐπὴν ὁ πατὴρ ὁ πελαργὸς ἐκπετησίμους   1355
πάντας ποιήσῃ τοὺς πελαργιδέας τρέφων,
δεῖ τοὺς νεοττοὺς τὸν πατέρα πάλιν τρέφειν.

ΠΑΤΡΑΛΟΙΑΣ
ἀπέλαυσά τἄρα νὴ Δί' ἐλθὼν ἐνθαδί,
εἴπερ γέ μοι καὶ τὸν πατέρα βοσκητέον.

ΠΙΣΘΕΤΑΙΡΟΣ
οὐδέν γ'. ἐπειδήπερ γὰρ ἦλθες ὦ μέλε   1360
εὔνους, πτερώσω σ' ὥσπερ ὄρνιν ὀρφανόν.
σοὶ δ' ὦ νεανίσκ' οὐ κακῶς ὑποθήσομαι,
ἀλλ' οἷάπερ αὐτὸς ἔμαθον ὅτε παῖς ἦ. σὺ γὰρ
τὸν μὲν πατέρα μὴ τύπτε· ταυτηνδὶ λαβὼν
τὴν πτέρυγα καὶ τουτὶ τὸ πλῆκτρον θἀτέρᾳ,   1365
νομίσας ἀλεκτρυόνος ἔχειν τονδὶ λόφον,
φρούρει στρατεύου μισθοφορῶν σαυτὸν τρέφε,
τὸν πατέρ ἔα ζῆν· ἀλλ' ἐπειδὴ μάχιμος εἶ,
ἐς τἀπὶ Θρᾴκης ἀποπέτου κἀκεῖ μάχου.

ΠΑΤΡΑΛΟΙΑΣ
νὴ τὸν Διόνυσον εὖ γέ μοι δοκεῖς λέγειν,   1370
καὶ πείσομαί σοι.

YOUNG MAN

> All of them—but I really like that one
> which says it's all right for a younger bird
> to beat up his old man and strangle him.

PISTHETAIROS

> Yes, by god, we think it very manly
> when a bird, while still a chick, beats up his dad.   [1350]

YOUNG MAN

> That's why I want to re-locate up here—
> I'd love to choke my father, get all his stuff.

PISTHETAIROS

> But there's an ancient law among the birds—
> inscribed in stone on tablets of the storks,
> "When father stork has raised up all his young,
> when they are set to fly out of the nest,
> then young storks must, in their turn, care for him."

YOUNG MAN

> So coming here has been no use, by god,
> if I've now got to feed my father, too.

PISTHETAIROS

> No, no. My dear young man, since you came here   [1360]
> in all good faith, I'll fix you up with wings
> just like an orphan bird.⁷⁵ And I'll give you
> some fresh advice—something I learned myself
> when I was just a lad. Don't thump your dad.

[Pisthetairos starts dressing the boy as a bird as he says the following lines]

> Take this wing here, and in your other hand
> hold this spur tight. Think of this crest on top
> as from a fighting cock. Then stand your guard,
> go on a march, live on a soldier's pay—
> and let your father live. You like to fight,
> so fly away to territories in Thrace,
> and do your fighting there.

YOUNG MAN

>   By Dionysus,
> I think the advice you give is good.   [1370]
> I'll do just what you say.

ΠΙΣΘΕΤΑΙΡΟΣ

Aristophanes

νοῦν ἄρ᾽ ἕξεις νὴ Δία.

ΚΙΝΗΣΙΑΣ

ἀναπέτομαι δὴ πρὸς Ὄλυμπον πτερύγεσσι κούφαις·
πέτομαι δ᾽ ὁδὸν ἄλλοτ᾽ ἐπ᾽ ἄλλαν μελέων —

ΠΙΣΘΕΤΑΙΡΟΣ

τουτὶ τὸ πρᾶγμα φορτίου δεῖται πτερῶν.   1375

ΚΙΝΗΣΙΑΣ

ἀφόβῳ φρενὶ σώματί τε νέαν ἐφέπων —

ΠΙΣΘΕΤΑΙΡΟΣ

ἀσπαζόμεσθα φιλύρινον Κινησίαν.
τί δεῦρο πόδα σὺ κυλλὸν ἀνὰ κύκλον κυκλεῖς;

ΚΙΝΗΣΙΑΣ

ὄρνις γενέσθαι βούλομαι λιγύφθογγος ἀηδών.   1380

ΠΙΣΘΕΤΑΙΡΟΣ

παῦσαι μελῳδῶν, ἀλλ᾽ ὅ τι λέγεις εἰπέ μοι.

ΚΙΝΗΣΙΑΣ

ὑπὸ σοῦ πτερωθεὶς βούλομαι μετάρσιος
ἀναπτόμενος ἐκ τῶν νεφελῶν καινὰς λαβεῖν
ἀεροδονήτους καὶ νιφοβόλους ἀναβολάς.   1385

ΠΙΣΘΕΤΑΙΡΟΣ

ἐκ τῶν νεφελῶν γὰρ ἄν τις ἀναβολὰς λάβοι;

ΚΙΝΗΣΙΑΣ

κρέμαται μὲν οὖν ἐντεῦθεν ἡμῶν ἡ τέχνη.
τῶν διθυράμβων γὰρ τὰ λαμπρὰ γίγνεται
ἀέρια καὶ σκότιά γε καὶ κυαναυγέα
καὶ πτεροδόνητα· σὺ δὲ κλύων εἴσει τάχα.   1390

ΠΙΣΘΕΤΑΙΡΟΣ

οὐ δῆτ᾽ ἔγωγε.

148

PISTHETAIROS

              And now, by Zeus,
you're talking sense.

[Exit Young Man. Enter Cinesias, singing and dancing very badly][76]

CINESIAS *[singing]*

              To Olympus on high
              with my wings I will fly —
              On this song's path I'll soar
              and then sing a few more . . .

PISTHETAIROS

This creature needs a whole pile of wings!

CINESIAS *[singing]*

              For my body and mind
              know not fear, so I'll find . . .

PISTHETAIROS

Cinesias, welcome. Let me now greet
a man as thin as bark on linden trees!
Why have you come whirling here on such lame feet?

CINESIAS

              A bird — that's what I long to be,   [1380]
              a clear-voice nightingale — that's me.

PISTHETAIROS

Stop singing — just tell me what you want to say.

CINESIAS

I want you to give me wings then float up,
flying high into the clouds where I can pluck
wind-whirling preludes swept with snow.

PISTHETAIROS

You want to get your preludes from the clouds?

CINESIAS

But all our skill depends upon the clouds.
Our brilliant dithyrambs are made of air —
of mist and gleaming murk and wispy wings.
You'll soon see that — once you've heard a few.   [1390]

PISTHETAIROS

No, no — I won't.

ΚΙΝΗΣΙΑΣ

νὴ τὸν Ἡρακλέα σύ γε.
ἅπαντα γὰρ δίειμί σοι τὸν ἀέρα.
εἴδωλα πετεινῶν
αἰθεροδρόμων
οἰωνῶν ταναοδείρων —

ΠΙΣΘΕΤΑΙΡΟΣ

ὠόπ.   1395

ΚΙΝΗΣΙΑΣ

τὸν ἀλάδρομον ἀλάμενος
ἅμ᾽ ἀνέμων πνοαῖσι βαίην.

ΠΙΣΘΕΤΑΙΡΟΣ

νὴ τὸν Δί᾽ ἢ ’γώ σου καταπαύσω τὰς πνοάς.

ΚΙΝΗΣΙΑΣ

τοτὲ μὲν νοτίαν στείχων πρὸς ὁδόν,
τοτὲ δ᾽ αὖ βορέᾳ σῶμα πελάζων
ἀλίμενον αἰθέρος αὔλακα τέμνων.   1400
χαρίεντά γ᾽ ὦ πρεσβῦτ᾽ ἐσοφίσω καὶ σοφά.

ΠΙΣΘΕΤΑΙΡΟΣ

οὐ γὰρ σὺ χαίρεις πτεροδόνητος γενόμενος;

ΚΙΝΗΣΙΑΣ

ταυτὶ πεποίηκας τὸν κυκλιοδιδάσκαλον,
ὃς ταῖσι φυλαῖς περιμάχητός εἰμ᾽ ἀεί;

ΠΙΣΘΕΤΑΙΡΟΣ

βούλει διδάσκειν καὶ παρ᾽ ἡμῖν οὖν μένων   1405
Λεωτροφίδῃ χορὸν πετομένων ὀρνέων
Κεκροπῖδα φυλήν;

ΚΙΝΗΣΙΑΣ

                    καταγελᾷς μου, δῆλος εἶ.
ἀλλ᾽ οὖν ἔγωγ᾽ οὐ παύσομαι, τοῦτ᾽ ἴσθ᾽ ὅτι,
πρὶν ἂν πτερωθεὶς διαδράμω τὸν ἀέρα.

CINESIAS
    Yes, by Hercules, you will.
For you I'll run through all the airs . . . *[starts singing]*

  O you images of birds,
  who extend your wings,
  who tread upon the air,
  you long-necked birds . . .

PISTHETAIROS *[trying to interrupt]*
  All right. Enough!

CINESIAS *[ignoring Pisthetairos, continuing to sing another song]*
  Soaring upward as I roam.
  I wander floating on the breeze . . .

PISTHETAIROS *[looking in one of the baskets of wings]*
  By heaven, I'll stop these blasting winds of yours!

[Pisthetairos takes a pair of wings and starts poking Cinesias around the stage with them, tickling him]

CINESIAS *[dodging away from Pisthetairos, giggling, and continuing to sing]*
  First I head along the highway going down south,
  but then my body turns towards the windy north,
  as I slice airy furrows where no harbour lies . . .   [1400]

[Cinesias has to stop singing because Pisthetairos is tickling him too much with the wings. He stops running off and singing. He's somewhat out of breath]

  Old man, that's a clever trick — pleasant, too —
  but really clever.

PISTHETAIROS
      You mean you don't enjoy
  being whisked with wings?

CINESIAS
      Is that the way you treat
  the man who trains the cyclic choruses —
  the one whom tribes of men still fight to have?[77]

PISTHETAIROS
  Would you like to stick around this place
  to train a chorus here for Leotrophides,[78]
  made up of flying birds — the swallow tribe?

CINESIAS
  You're making fun of me — that's obvious.
  But I won't stop here until I get some wings
  and I can run through all the airs.

ΣΥΚΟΦΑΝΤΗΣ
ὄρνιθες τίνες οὐδὲν ἔχοντες πτεροποίκιλοι,　　　1410
τανυσίπτερε ποικίλα χελιδοῖ;

ΠΙΣΘΕΤΑΙΡΟΣ
τουτὶ τὸ κακὸν οὐ φαῦλον ἐξεγρήγορεν.
ὅδ' αὖ μινυρίζων δεῦρό τις προσέρχεται.

ΣΥΚΟΦΑΝΤΗΣ
τανυσίπτερε ποικίλα μάλ' αὖθις.　　　1415

ΠΙΣΘΕΤΑΙΡΟΣ
ἐς θοἰμάτιον τὸ σκόλιον ᾄδειν μοι δοκεῖ,
δεῖσθαι δ' ἔοικεν οὐκ ὀλίγων χελιδόνων.

ΣΥΚΟΦΑΝΤΗΣ
τίς ὁ πτερῶν δεῦρ' ἐστὶ τοὺς ἀφικνουμένους;

ΠΙΣΘΕΤΑΙΡΟΣ
ὁδὶ πάρεστιν· ἀλλ' ὅτου δεῖ χρὴ λέγειν.

ΣΥΚΟΦΑΝΤΗΣ
πτερῶν πτερῶν δεῖ· μὴ πύθῃ τὸ δεύτερον.　　　1420

ΠΙΣΘΕΤΑΙΡΟΣ
μῶν εὐθὺ Πελλήνης πέτεσθαι διανοεῖ;

ΣΥΚΟΦΑΝΤΗΣ
μὰ Δί' ἀλλὰ κλητήρ εἰμι νησιωτικὸς
καὶ συκοφάντης —

ΠΙΣΘΕΤΑΙΡΟΣ
　　　　　　ὦ μακάριε τῆς τέχνης.

ΣΥΚΟΦΑΝΤΗΣ
καὶ πραγματοδίφης. εἶτα δέομαι πτερὰ λαβὼν
κύκλῳ περισοβεῖν τὰς πόλεις καλούμενος.　　　1425

[Exit Cinesias. Enter a Sycophant, singing to himself]

SYCOPHANT *[singing]*
>   Who are these birds with mottled wing?   [1410]
>   They don't appear to own a thing—
>   O dappled swallow with extended wing . . .

PISTHETAIROS
>   This is no minor problem we've stirred up—
>   here comes one more person singing to himself.

SYCOPHANT *[singing]*
>   O long and dappled wings, I call once more . . .

PISTHETAIROS
>   It seems to me his song's about his cloak—
>   he needs a lot of swallows to bring in the spring.[79]

SYCOPHANT
>   Where's the man who's handing out the wings
>   to all who travel here?

PISTHETAIROS
>   He's standing here.
>   But you should tell me what you need.

SYCOPHANT
>   Wings, wings.
>   I need wings. Don't ask me that again.   [1420]

PISTHETAIROS
>   Do you intend to fly off right away,
>   heading for Pellene?

SYCOPHANT
>   No, not at all.
>   I'm a summons server for the islands—
>   an informer, too . . .

PISTHETAIROS
>   You're a lucky man
>   to have such a fine profession.

SYCOPHANT
>   . . . and I hunt around
>   to dig up law suits. That's why I need wings,
>   to roam around delivering summonses
>   in allied states.

ΠΙΣΘΕΤΑΙΡΟΣ
ὑπὸ πτερύγων τι προσκαλεῖ σοφώτερον;

ΣΥΚΟΦΑΝΤΗΣ
μὰ Δί' ἀλλ' ἵν' οἱ λῃσταί τε μὴ λυπῶσί με,
μετὰ τῶν γεράνων τ' ἐκεῖθεν ἀναχωρῶ πάλιν,
ἀνθ' ἕρματος πολλὰς καταπεπωκὼς δίκας.

ΠΙΣΘΕΤΑΙΡΟΣ
τουτὶ γὰρ ἐργάζει σὺ τοὔργον; εἰπέ μοι,   1430
νεανίας ὢν συκοφαντεῖς τοὺς ξένους;

ΣΥΚΟΦΑΝΤΗΣ
τί γὰρ πάθω; σκάπτειν γὰρ οὐκ ἐπίσταμαι.

ΠΙΣΘΕΤΑΙΡΟΣ
ἀλλ' ἔστιν ἕτερα νὴ Δί' ἔργα σώφρονα,
ἀφ' ὧν διαζῆν ἄνδρα χρῆν τοσουτονὶ
ἐκ τοῦ δικαίου μᾶλλον ἢ δικορραφεῖν.   1435

ΣΥΚΟΦΑΝΤΗΣ
ὦ δαιμόνιε μὴ νουθέτει μ' ἀλλὰ πτέρου.

ΠΙΣΘΕΤΑΙΡΟΣ
νῦν τοι λέγων πτερῶ σε.

ΣΥΚΟΦΑΝΤΗΣ
                                   καὶ πῶς ἂν λόγοις
ἄνδρα πτερώσειας σύ;

ΠΙΣΘΕΤΑΙΡΟΣ
                                    πάντες τοῖς λόγοις
ἀναπτεροῦνται.

ΣΥΚΟΦΑΝΤΗΣ
                         πάντες;

ΠΙΣΘΕΤΑΙΡΟΣ
                                     οὐκ ἀκήκοας,
ὅταν λέγωσιν οἱ πατέρες ἑκάστοτε   1440
τοῖς μειρακίοις ἐν τοῖσι κουρείοις ταδί;
'δεινῶς γέ μου τὸ μειράκιον Διειτρέφης
λέγων ἀνεπτέρωκεν ὥσθ' ἱππηλατεῖν.'

PISTHETAIROS

If you're equipped with wings,
will that make you more skilled in serving men?

SYCOPHANT

No. But I'd escape being hurt by pirates.
And then I could return home with the cranes,
once I've swallowed many law suits down
to serve as ballast.[80]

PISTHETAIROS

Is that what you do for work?   [1430]
Tell me this — you're a strong young lad and yet
don't you slander strangers for a living?

SYCOPHANT

What can I do? I never learned to dig.

PISTHETAIROS

But, by god, there are other decent jobs,
where a young man like you can earn his way,
more honest trades than launching still more law suits.

SYCOPHANT

My good man, don't keep lecturing me like this.
Give me some wings.

PISTHETAIROS

I'm giving you some wings —
I'm doing it as I talk to you right now.

SYCOPHANT

How can you put wings on men with words?

PISTHETAIROS

With words all men can give themselves their wings.

SYCOPHANT

All men?

PISTHETAIROS

Have you never heard in barber shops
how fathers always talk of their young sons —   [1440]
"It's dreadful the way that Diitrephes' speech
has given my young lad ambitious wings,
so now he wants to race his chariot."

ὁ δέ τις τὸν αὑτοῦ φησιν ἐπὶ τραγῳδίᾳ
ἀνεπτερῶσθαι καὶ πεποτῆσθαι τὰς φρένας.　　1445

ΣΥΚΟΦΑΝΤΗΣ

λόγοισί τἄρα καὶ πτεροῦνται;

ΠΙΣΘΕΤΑΙΡΟΣ

　　　　　　　　φήμ᾽ ἐγώ.
ὑπὸ γὰρ λόγων ὁ νοῦς τε μετεωρίζεται
ἐπαίρεταί τ᾽ ἄνθρωπος. οὕτω καί σ᾽ ἐγὼ
ἀναπτερώσας βούλομαι χρηστοῖς λόγοις
τρέψαι πρὸς ἔργον νόμιμον.　　1450

ΣΥΚΟΦΑΝΤΗΣ

　　　　　　　ἀλλ᾽ οὐ βούλομαι.

ΠΙΣΘΕΤΑΙΡΟΣ

τί δαὶ ποιήσεις;

ΣΥΚΟΦΑΝΤΗΣ

　　　　　τὸ γένος οὐ καταισχυνῶ.
παππῷος ὁ βίος συκοφαντεῖν ἐστί μοι.
ἀλλὰ πτέρου με ταχέσι καὶ κούφοις πτεροῖς
ἱέρακος ἢ κερχνῇδος, ὡς ἂν τοὺς ξένους
καλεσάμενος κᾆτ᾽ ἐγκεκληκὼς ἐνθαδὶ　　1455
κατ᾽ αὖ πέτωμαι πάλιν ἐκεῖσε.

ΠΙΣΘΕΤΑΙΡΟΣ

　　　　　　　μανθάνω.
ὡδὶ λέγεις· ὅπως ἂν ὠφλήκῃ δίκην
ἐνθάδε πρὶν ἥκειν ὁ ξένος.

ΣΥΚΟΦΑΝΤΗΣ

　　　　　　πάνυ μανθάνεις.

ΠΙΣΘΕΤΑΙΡΟΣ

κἄπειθ᾽ ὁ μὲν πλεῖ δεῦρο, σὺ δ᾽ ἐκεῖσ᾽ αὖ πέτει
ἁρπασόμενος τὰ χρήματ᾽ αὐτοῦ.

ΣΥΚΟΦΑΝΤΗΣ

　　　　　　　πάντ᾽ ἔχεις.　　1460
βέμβικος οὐδὲν διαφέρειν δεῖ.

Another says "That boy of mine has wings
and flutters over tragedies."

SYCOPHANT

So with words
they're really given wings?

PISTHETAIROS

That what I said.
With words our minds are raised—a man can soar.
That's how I want to give you wings—with words,
with useful words, so you can change your life
and get a lawful occupation.

SYCOPHANT

But I don't want to.   [1450]

PISTHETAIROS

What will you do?

SYCOPHANT

I'll not disgrace my folks.
Informing—that's my family's profession.
So give me now some light, fast falcon's wings—
or kestrel's—then I can serve my papers
on those foreigners, lay the charges here,
and fly back there again.

PISTHETAIROS

Ah, I get it—
what you're saying is that the case is judged
before the stranger gets here.

SYCOPHANT

That's right.
You understand exactly what I do.

PISTHETAIROS

And then, while he's travelling here by ship,
you fly out there to seize his property.

SYCOPHANT

You've said it all. I've got to whip around   [1460]
just like a whirling top.

ΠΙΣΘΕΤΑΙΡΟΣ

μανθάνω
βέμβικα· καὶ μὴν ἔστι μοι νὴ τὸν Δία
κάλλιστα Κορκυραῖα τοιαυτὶ πτερά.

ΣΥΚΟΦΑΝΤΗΣ

οἴμοι τάλας μάστιγ᾽ ἔχεις.

ΠΙΣΘΕΤΑΙΡΟΣ

πτερὼ μὲν οὖν,
οἷσί σε ποιήσω τήμερον βεμβικιᾶν.   1465

ΣΥΚΟΦΑΝΤΗΣ

οἴμοι τάλας.

ΠΙΣΘΕΤΑΙΡΟΣ

οὐ πτερυγιεῖς ἐντευθενί;
οὐκ ἀπολιβάξεις ὦ κάκιστ᾽ ἀπολούμενος;
πικρὰν τάχ᾽ ὄψει στρεψοδικοπανουργίαν.
ἀπίωμεν ἡμεῖς ξυλλαβόντες τὰ πτερά.

ΧΟΡΟΣ

πολλὰ δὴ καὶ καινὰ καὶ θαυμάστ᾽   1470
ἐπεπτόμεσθα καὶ
δεινὰ πράγματ᾽ εἴδομεν.
ἔστι γὰρ δένδρον πεφυκὸς
ἔκτοπόν τι Καρδίας ἀ-
πωτέρω Κλεώνυμος,   1475
χρήσιμον μὲν οὐδέν, ἄλλως
δὲ δειλὸν καὶ μέγα.
τοῦτο τοῦ μὲν ἦρος ἀεὶ
βλαστάνει καὶ συκοφαντεῖ,
τοῦ δὲ χειμῶνος πάλιν τὰς   1480
ἀσπίδας φυλλορροεῖ.

158

PISTHETAIROS

I understand—
a whirling top. Well, here, by god, I've got
the finest wings. They're from Corcyra . . . here!

[Pisthetairos produces a whip from the basket and begins hitting the Syco-phant, who dodges around to evade the blows]

SYCOPHANT

Ouch! That's a whip you've got!

PISTHETAIROS

No—a pair of wings.
With them I'll make you spin around all day!

SYCOPHANT

Ow! Help! That hurts!

PISTHETAIROS

Wing your way from here!
Get lost—I want rid of you, you rascal!
I'll show you legal tricks and twists—sharp ones, too!

[Pisthetairos beats the Sycophant off stage. Enter Xanthias and Man-odorus from the house]

Let's gather up these wings and go inside.

[Pisthetairos and the two slaves carry the baskets of wings back into the house]

CHORUS

When we fly   [1470]
we often spy
strange amazing spots—
in those flights
peculiar sights.

There's a tree grows far from us
simply called Cleonymos,
a useless tree, without a heart—
immense, and vile in every part.
It always blooms in early spring,
bursting forth with everything
that launches legal quarrelling.
and then in winter time it yields   [1480]
a shedding foliage of shields.

Aristophanes

ἔστι δ' αὖ χώρα πρὸς αὐτῷ
τῷ σκότῳ πόρρω τις ἐν
τῇ λύχνων ἐρημίᾳ,
ἔνθα τοῖς ἥρωσιν ἄνθρωποι   1485
ξυναριστῶσι καὶ ξύνεισι
πλὴν τῆς ἑσπέρας.
τηνικαῦτα δ' οὐκέτ' ἦν
ἀσφαλὲς ξυντυγχάνειν.
εἰ γὰρ ἐντύχοι τις ἥρῳ   1490
τῶν βροτῶν νύκτωρ Ὀρέστῃ,
γυμνὸς ἦν πληγεὶς ὑπ' αὐτοῦ
πάντα τἀπιδέξια.

ΠΡΟΜΗΘΕΥΣ
οἴμοι τάλας, ὁ Ζεὺς ὅπως μή μ' ὄψεται.
ποῦ Πισθέταιρός ἐστ';

ΠΙΣΘΕΤΑΙΡΟΣ
                              ἔα τουτὶ τί ἦν;   1495
τίς ὁ συγκαλυμμός;

ΠΡΟΜΗΘΕΥΣ
                              τῶν θεῶν ὁρᾷς τινα
ἐμοῦ κατόπιν ἐνταῦθα;

ΠΙΣΘΕΤΑΙΡΟΣ
                              μὰ Δί' ἐγὼ μὲν οὔ.
τίς δ' εἶ σύ;

ΠΡΟΜΗΘΕΥΣ
                              πηνίκ' ἐστὶν ἄρα τῆς ἡμέρας;

ΠΙΣΘΕΤΑΙΡΟΣ
ὁπηνίκα; σμικρόν τι μετὰ μεσημβρίαν.
ἀλλὰ σὺ τίς εἶ;

ΠΡΟΜΗΘΕΥΣ
                              βουλυτὸς ἢ περαιτέρω;   1500

ΠΙΣΘΕΤΑΙΡΟΣ
οἴμ' ὡς βδελύττομαί σε.

160

There's a land
ringed by the dark,
a gloomy wilderness,
where Heroes meet
and with men eat.

Men live with heroes in that place,
except at dusk — then it's not safe
for the two of them to meet.
Men who in the night time greet   [1490]
the great Orestes are stripped bare
he strikes at them and leaves them there.
And so without their clothes they bide —
paralysed on their right side.[81]

[Enter Prometheus, muffling his face in a long scarf and holding an unopened umbrella]

PROMETHEUS
    Oh, dear, dear, dear. I pray Zeus doesn't see me.
    Where's Pisthetairos?

[Pisthetairos enters from the house carrying a chamber pot. He is surprised to see the new arrival]

PISTHETAIROS
           Who's this? Why so muffled?

PROMETHEUS
    Do you see any god who's trailed me here?

PISTHETAIROS
    No, by Zeus, I don't. But who are you?

PROMETHEUS
    What time of day is it?

PISTHETAIROS
           What time of day?
    A little after noon. But who are you?

PROMETHEUS
    Quitting time or later?   [1500]

PISTHETAIROS
           You're pissing me off . . .

ΠΡΟΜΗΘΕΥΣ

τί γὰρ ὁ Ζεὺς ποιεῖ;
ἀπαιθριάζει τὰς νεφέλας ἢ ξυννέφει;

ΠΙΣΘΕΤΑΙΡΟΣ
οἴμωζε μεγάλ'.

ΠΡΟΜΗΘΕΥΣ
οὕτω μὲν ἐκκεκαλύψομαι.

ΠΙΣΘΕΤΑΙΡΟΣ
ὦ φίλε Προμηθεῦ.

ΠΡΟΜΗΘΕΥΣ
παῦε παῦε, μὴ βόα.

ΠΙΣΘΕΤΑΙΡΟΣ
τί γὰρ ἔστι;   1505

ΠΡΟΜΗΘΕΥΣ
σίγα, μὴ κάλει μου τοὔνομα·
ἀπὸ γάρ μ' ὀλεῖς, εἴ μ' ἐνθάδ' ὁ Ζεὺς ὄψεται.
ἀλλ' ἵνα φράσω σοι πάντα τἄνω πράγματα,
τουτὶ λαβών μου τὸ σκιάδειον ὑπέρεχε
ἄνωθεν, ὡς ἂν μή μ' ὁρῶσιν οἱ θεοί.

ΠΙΣΘΕΤΑΙΡΟΣ
ἰοὺ ἰού·   1510
εὖ γ' ἐπενόησας αὐτὸ καὶ προμηθικῶς.
ὑπόδυθι ταχὺ δὴ κᾆτα θαρρήσας λέγε.

ΠΡΟΜΗΘΕΥΣ
ἄκουε δή νυν.

ΠΙΣΘΕΤΑΙΡΟΣ
ὡς ἀκούοντος λέγε.

ΠΡΟΜΗΘΕΥΣ
ἀπόλωλεν ὁ Ζεύς.

ΠΙΣΘΕΤΑΙΡΟΣ
πηνίκ' ἄττ' ἀπώλετο;

PROMETHEUS

    What's Zeus up to? What about the clouds—
    is he scattering 'em—or bringing 'em together?

PISTHETAIROS

    You're a total fool!

PROMETHEUS

              All right—then I'll unwrap.

[Prometheus takes off the muffler concealing his face]

PISTHETAIROS

    Prometheus, my friend!

PROMETHEUS

              Hey, quiet. Don't shout.

PISTHETAIROS

    What's the matter?

PROMETHEUS

              Shhh . . . don't shout my name.
    I'm done for if Zeus can see I'm here.
    But I'll tell you what's going on up there,
    if you take this umbrella. Hold it up,
    above our heads—that way no god can see.

PISTHETAIROS

    Ah ha! Now that's a smart precaution—   [1510]
    that's forethought, just like Prometheus!
    Come under here—make it fast—all right, now,
    you can talk without a worry.

[Pisthetairos and Prometheus huddle together under the umbrella]

PROMETHEUS

              Then listen.

PISTHETAIROS

    I'm listening—speak up.

PROMETHEUS

              Zeus is done for.

PISTHETAIROS

    And when was he done in?

Aristophanes

ΠΡΟΜΗΘΕΥΣ
ἐξ οὗπερ ὑμεῖς ᾠκίσατε τὸν ἀέρα.   1515
θύει γὰρ οὐδεὶς οὐδὲν ἀνθρώπων ἔτι
θεοῖσιν, οὐδὲ κνῖσα μηρίων ἄπο
ἀνῆλθεν ὡς ἡμᾶς ἀπ' ἐκείνου τοῦ χρόνου,
ἀλλ' ὡσπερεὶ Θεσμοφορίοις νηστεύομεν
ἄνευ θυηλῶν· οἱ δὲ βάρβαροι θεοὶ   1520
πεινῶντες ὥσπερ Ἰλλυριοὶ κεκριγότες
ἐπιστρατεύσειν φάσ' ἄνωθεν τῷ Διί,
εἰ μὴ παρέξει τἀμπόρι' ἀνεῳγμένα,
ἵν' εἰσάγοιτο σπλάγχνα κατατετμημένα.

ΠΙΣΘΕΤΑΙΡΟΣ
εἰσὶν γὰρ ἕτεροι βάρβαροι θεοί τινες   1525
ἄνωθεν ὑμῶν;

ΠΡΟΜΗΘΕΥΣ
οὐ γάρ εἰσι βάρβαροι,
ὅθεν ὁ πατρῷός ἐστιν Ἐξηκεστίδῃ;

ΠΙΣΘΕΤΑΙΡΟΣ
ὄνομα δὲ τούτοις τοῖς θεοῖς τοῖς βαρβάροις
τί ἔστιν;

ΠΡΟΜΗΘΕΥΣ
ὅ τι ἔστιν; Τριβαλλοί.

ΠΙΣΘΕΤΑΙΡΟΣ
                              μανθάνω.
ἐντεῦθεν ἆρα τοὐπιτριβείης ἐγένετο;   1530

ΠΡΟΜΗΘΕΥΣ
μάλιστα πάντων. ἓν δέ σοι λέγω σαφές·
ἥξουσι πρέσβεις δεῦρο περὶ διαλλαγῶν
παρὰ τοῦ Διὸς καὶ τῶν Τριβαλλῶν τῶν ἄνω·
ὑμεῖς δὲ μὴ σπένδεσθ', ἐὰν μὴ παραδιδῷ
τὸ σκῆπτρον ὁ Ζεὺς τοῖσιν ὄρνισιν πάλιν,   1535
καὶ τὴν Βασίλειάν σοι γυναῖκ' ἔχειν διδῷ.

ΠΙΣΘΕΤΑΙΡΟΣ
τίς ἐστιν ἡ Βασίλεια;

164

PROMETHEUS

                                      It happened
once you colonized the air. From that point on,
no human being has made a sacrifice
to any god, not once—and since that time
no savoury smells from roasting thigh bones
have risen up to us from down below.
So now, without our offerings, we must fast,
as if it's time for Thesmophoria.[82]
The barbarian gods are starving—so now   [1520]
they scream out like Illyrians and say
their armies will march down attacking Zeus,
unless he moves to get the ports re-opened,
to make sliced entrails once again available.

PISTHETAIROS
You mean other gods, barbarian ones,
are there above you?

PROMETHEUS
Barbarian deities? Of course.
That's where Execestides derives
all his ancestral family gods.

PISTHETAIROS
What's the name of these barbarian gods?

PROMETHEUS
The name? They're called Triballians.[83]

PISTHETAIROS
I see—that must be where we get our phrase
they've got me "by the balls."   [1530]

PROMETHEUS
                         You got that right.
Now let me tell you something to the point—
ambassadors are coming here to settle this,
from Zeus and those Triballians up there.
But don't agree to peace unless great Zeus
gives back his sceptre to the birds again,
and gives the Princess to you as your wife.

PISTHETAIROS
Whose this Princess?

ΠΡΟΜΗΘΕΥΣ

καλλίστη κόρη,
ἥπερ ταμιεύει τὸν κεραυνὸν τοῦ Διὸς
καὶ τἄλλ᾽ ἀπαξάπαντα, τὴν εὐβουλίαν
τὴν εὐνομίαν τὴν σωφροσύνην τὰ νεώρια,   1540
τὴν λοιδορίαν τὸν κωλακρέτην τὰ τριώβολα.

ΠΙΣΘΕΤΑΙΡΟΣ

ἅπαντά γ᾽ ἆρ᾽ αὐτῷ ταμιεύει;

ΠΡΟΜΗΘΕΥΣ

φήμ᾽ ἐγώ.
ἥν γ᾽ ἢν σὺ παρ᾽ ἐκείνου παραλάβῃς, πάντ᾽ ἔχεις.
τούτων ἕνεκα δεῦρ᾽ ἦλθον, ἵνα φράσαιμί σοι.
ἀεί ποτ᾽ ἀνθρώποις γὰρ εὔνους εἴμ᾽ ἐγώ.   1545

ΠΙΣΘΕΤΑΙΡΟΣ

μόνον θεῶν γὰρ διὰ σ᾽ ἀπανθρακίζομεν.

ΠΡΟΜΗΘΕΥΣ

μισῶ δ᾽ ἅπαντας τοὺς θεούς, ὡς οἶσθα σύ.

ΠΙΣΘΕΤΑΙΡΟΣ

νὴ τὸν Δί᾽ ἀεὶ δῆτα θεομισὴς ἔφυς.

ΠΡΟΜΗΘΕΥΣ

Τίμων καθαρός. ἀλλ᾽ ὡς ἂν ἀποτρέχω πάλιν,
φέρε τὸ σκιάδειον, ἵνα με κἂν ὁ Ζεὺς ἴδῃ   1550
ἄνωθεν, ἀκολουθεῖν δοκῶ κανηφόρῳ.

ΠΙΣΘΕΤΑΙΡΟΣ

καὶ τὸν δίφρον γε διφροφόρει τονδὶ λαβών.

ΧΟΡΟΣ

πρὸς δὲ τοῖς Σκιάποσιν λί-
μνη τις ἔστ᾽ ἄλουτος οὗ
ψυχαγωγεῖ Σωκράτης·   1555

166

PROMETHEUS
                        The loveliest of girls—
she's the one in charge of Zeus' thunderbolt
and all his assets—wise advice, good laws,
sound common sense, dockyards, slanderous talk—   [1540]
his paymistress who hands three obols out
to jury men . . .

PISTHETAIROS
                        So in Zeus' name,
she's the one in charge of everything?

PROMETHEUS
                        That's right.
If you get her from Zeus, you've got it all.
That's why I came here to tell you this.
I've always been a friend of human beings.

PISTHETAIROS
Yes, of all the gods it's thanks to you
that we can fry up fish.[84]

PROMETHEUS
                        I hate all gods—
but you know that.

PISTHETAIROS
                        You've always hated them.
Heaven knows—it's something natural to you.

PROMETHEUS
I'm Timon through and through.[85] Time to get back.
So let me have the parasol. That way,
if Zeus does catch sight of me from there,   [1550]
he'll think I'm following some basket girl.

PISTHETAIROS
Take the piss pot, too—then you can act
as if you're the one who's carrying the stool.

[Prometheus leaves with the umbrella and the pot. Pisthetairos goes back into the house]

CHORUS
By that tribe of men with such huge feet
they use them for a shade retreat,
there's stands a lake where Socrates,
deceives men's souls, that unwashed tease.

Aristophanes

ἔνθα καὶ Πείσανδρος ἦλθε
δεόμενος ψυχὴν ἰδεῖν ἣ
ζῶντ᾽ ἐκεῖνον προὔλιπε,
σφάγι᾽ ἔχων κάμηλον ἀ-
μνόν τιν᾽, ἧς λαιμοὺς τεμὼν ὥσ-   1560
περ ποθ᾽ οὑδυσσεὺς ἀπῆλθε,
κᾆτ᾽ ἀνῆλθ᾽ αὐτῷ κάτωθεν
πρὸς τὸ λαῖτμα τῆς καμήλου
Χαιρεφῶν ἡ νυκτερίς.

ΠΟΣΕΙΔΩΝ

τὸ μὲν πόλισμα τῆς Νεφελοκοκκυγίας   1565
ὁρᾶν τοδὶ πάρεστιν, οἷ πρεσβεύομεν.
οὗτος τί δρᾷς; ἐπ᾽ ἀριστέρ᾽ οὕτως ἀμπέχει;
οὐ μεταβαλεῖς θοἰμάτιον ὧδ᾽ ἐπιδέξια;
τί ὦ κακόδαιμον; Λαισποδίας εἶ τὴν φύσιν;
ὦ δημοκρατία ποῖ προβιβᾷς ἡμᾶς ποτε,   1570
εἰ τουτονί γ᾽ ἐχειροτόνησαν οἱ θεοί;
ἕξεις ἀτρέμας; οἴμωζε· πολὺ γὰρ δή σ᾽ ἐγὼ
ἑόρακα πάντων βαρβαρώτατον θεῶν.
ἄγε δὴ τί δρῶμεν Ἡράκλεις;

ΗΡΑΚΛΗΣ

                                          ἀκήκοας
ἐμοῦ γ᾽ ὅτι τὸν ἄνθρωπον ἄγχειν βούλομαι,   1575
ὅστις ποτ᾽ ἔσθ᾽ ὁ τοὺς θεοὺς ἀποτειχίσας.

ΠΟΣΕΙΔΩΝ

ἀλλ᾽ ὦγάθ᾽ ᾑρήμεσθα περὶ διαλλαγῶν
πρέσβεις.

ΗΡΑΚΛΗΣ

        διπλασίως μᾶλλον ἄγχειν μοι δοκεῖ.

Peisander went there to find out
the spirit his life had been without.
A big young camel he did slay, [1560]
then, like Odysseus, snuck away.
By camel's blood to that place drawn,
up pops a Bat—it's Chaerephon![86]

[Enter Poseidon, Hercules, and the Triballian god]

POSEIDON
Here it is—Cloudcuckooland—in plain view,
city we've come to as ambassadors.

[Poseidon inspects the clothing on the Triballian god]

What *are* you doing? Why drape your cloak that way,
from right to left? It's got to be re-slung
the other way—like this.

[The Triballian tries to reshape his cloak but gets in a mess]

You fumbling idiot—
a born Laespodias, that's what you are![87]
O democracy! Where are you taking us, [1570]
when gods vote in a clumsy oaf like this?

[Poseidon continues to fuss over the Triballian's appearance]

Keep your hands still! Oh, to hell with you!
You're the most uncivilized of all the gods
I've ever seen. All right, Hercules,
what do we do?

HERCULES
You've heard what I propose.
I'd like to wring his neck—whoever he is
who set up this blockade against the gods.

POSEIDON
But you forget, my friend, that we've been sent
as envoys to negotiate down here.

HERCULES
That just makes me want to throttle him
twice as much as I wanted to before.

*[The wall of the house now moves off to reveal Pisthetairos and the slaves
getting dinner ready. They are preparing birds to cook in the oven]*

ΠΙΣΘΕΤΑΙΡΟΣ
τὴν τυρόκνηστίν τις δότω· φέρε σίλφιον·
τυρὸν φερέτω τις· πυρπόλει τοὺς ἄνθρακας.　　1580

ΠΟΣΕΙΔΩΝ
τὸν ἄνδρα χαίρειν οἱ θεοὶ κελεύομεν
τρεῖς ὄντες ἡμεῖς.

ΠΙΣΘΕΤΑΙΡΟΣ
　　　　　　ἀλλ' ἐπικνῶ τὸ σίλφιον.

ἩΡΑΚΛΗΣ
τὰ δὲ κρέα τοῦ ταῦτ' ἐστίν;

ΠΙΣΘΕΤΑΙΡΟΣ
　　　　　　　　ὄρνιθές τινες
ἐπανιστάμενοι τοῖς δημοτικοῖσιν ὀρνέοις
ἔδοξαν ἀδικεῖν.　　1585

ἩΡΑΚΛΗΣ
　　　　　εἶτα δῆτα σίλφιον
εἴπικνῆς πρότερον αὐτοῖσιν;

ΠΙΣΘΕΤΑΙΡΟΣ
　　　　　　　ὦ χαῖρ' Ἡράκλεις.
τί ἔστι;

ΠΟΣΕΙΔΩΝ
πρεσβεύοντες ἡμεῖς ἥκομεν
παρὰ τῶν θεῶν περὶ πολέμου καταλλαγῆς.

ΠΙΣΘΕΤΑΙΡΟΣ
ἔλαιον οὐκ ἔνεστιν ἐν τῇ ληκύθῳ.

ἩΡΑΚΛΗΣ
καὶ μὴν τά γ' ὀρνίθεια λιπάρ' εἶναι πρέπει.　　1590

ΠΟΣΕΙΔΩΝ
ἡμεῖς τε γὰρ πολεμοῦντες οὐ κερδαίνομεν,
ὑμεῖς τ' ἂν ἡμῖν τοῖς θεοῖς ὄντες φίλοι
ὄμβριον ὕδωρ ἂν εἴχετ' ἐν τοῖς τέλμασιν,
ἀλκυονίδας τ' ἂν ἦγεθ' ἡμέρας ἀεί.
τούτων περὶ πάντων αὐτοκράτορες ἥκομεν.　　1595

PISTHETAIROS
>The grater for the cheese—can someone get it?
>And bring the silphium. Hand me the cheese.
>Now, fire up the coals. [1580]

POSEIDON
>>Greetings, mortal.
>We three are gods, and we salute you!

PISTHETAIROS
>But I'm grating silphium right now.

HERCULES
>What kind of meat is this?

PISTHETAIROS
>>The meat's from birds—
>they've been tried and sentenced for rebellion,
>rising up against the fowl democracy.

HERCULES
>Is that why you're shredding silphium
>all over them before doing something else?

PISTHETAIROS *[looking up and recognizing Hercules]*
>Well, hello there, Hercules. What's up?

POSEIDON
>We've come as envoys sent down from the gods
>to negotiate the terms for peace.

PISTHETAIROS *[to one of the slaves]*
>There's no oil left in the jug.

HERCULES
>>And bird meat
>should be glistening with lots of oil. [1590]

POSEIDON
>We gods get no advantage from this war.
>If you and yours were friendly to the gods,
>you'd have water from the rain in all your ponds—
>halcyon days would be here all the time.
>We've come with total powers in such things.

ΠΙΣΘΕΤΑΙΡΟΣ
ἀλλ' οὔτε πρότερον πώποθ' ἡμεῖς ἤρξαμεν
πολέμου πρὸς ὑμᾶς, νῦν τ' ἐθέλομεν, εἰ δοκεῖ,
ἐάν τι δίκαιον ἀλλὰ νῦν ἐθέλητε δρᾶν,
σπονδὰς ποιεῖσθαι. τὰ δὲ δίκαι' ἐστὶν ταδί,
τὸ σκῆπτρον ἡμῖν τοῖσιν ὄρνισιν πάλιν   1600
τὸν Δί' ἀποδοῦναι· κἂν διαλλαττώμεθα
ἐπὶ τοῖσδε, τοὺς πρέσβεις ἐπ' ἄριστον καλῶ.

ΗΡΑΚΛΗΣ
ἐμοὶ μὲν ἀπόχρη ταῦτα καὶ ψηφίζομαι.

ΠΟΣΕΙΔΩΝ
τί ὦ κακόδαιμον; ἠλίθιος καὶ γάστρις εἶ.
ἀποστερεῖς τὸν πατέρα τῆς τυραννίδος;   1605

ΠΙΣΘΕΤΑΙΡΟΣ
ἄληθες; οὐ γὰρ μεῖζον ὑμεῖς οἱ θεοὶ
ἰσχύσετ', ἢν ὄρνιθες ἄρξωσιν κάτω;
νῦν μέν γ' ὑπὸ ταῖς νεφέλαισιν ἐγκεκρυμμένοι
κύψαντες ἐπιορκοῦσιν ὑμᾶς οἱ βροτοί·
ἐὰν δὲ τοὺς ὄρνις ἔχητε συμμάχους,   1610
ὅταν ὀμνύῃ τις τὸν κόρακα καὶ τὸν Δία,
ὁ κόραξ παρελθὼν τοὐπιορκοῦντος λάθρα
προσπτόμενος ἐκκόψει τὸν ὀφθαλμὸν θενών.

ΠΟΣΕΙΔΩΝ
νὴ τὸν Ποσειδῶ ταῦτά γέ τοι καλῶς λέγεις.

ΗΡΑΚΛΗΣ
κἀμοὶ δοκεῖ.   1615

ΠΙΣΘΕΤΑΙΡΟΣ
            τί δαὶ σὺ φής;

ΤΡΙΒΑΛΛΟΣ
                        ναβαισατρεῦ.

ΠΙΣΘΕΤΑΙΡΟΣ
ὁρᾷς; ἐπαινεῖ χοὖτος. ἕτερόν νυν ἔτι
ἀκούσαθ' ὅσον ὑμᾶς ἀγαθὸν ποιήσομεν.
ἐάν τις ἀνθρώπων ἱερεῖόν τῳ θεῶν

PISTHETAIROS
From the start we didn't launch a war on you—
and we're ready to talk peace, if that's your wish,
provided you're prepared to do what's right.
And here's what's right: Zeus gives his sceptre back
to us—I mean the birds—once more. And then,
if we can settle this on these conditions,
I'll invite the envoys to have lunch with me.

HERCULES *[salivating over the prepared bird]*
That's just fine with me! I vote we say . . .

POSEIDON *[interrupting]*
What's that you fool! Idiotic glutton!
You want give away your father's power? [1600]

PISTHETAIROS
Is that what you think? Look, if birds here
rule everything down there, won't you gods above
be even stronger? Now underneath the clouds
men can bend down and swear false oaths to you.
But once the birds and you become allies, [1610]
if any man should swear by Raven and by Zeus
and then perjure himself, Raven would come by,
swoop down upon the man before he sees him,
peck at his eye and pluck it out.

POSEIDON
                    By Poseidon,
what you're saying makes good sense!

HERCULES
                    Sounds good to me.

PISTHETAIROS *[to the Triballian god]*
What do you say?

TRIBALLIAN *[speaking foreign gibberish]*
                    Nab aist roo.

PISTHETAIROS
You hear what he said? He agrees with you.
Now listen up—here's yet another benefit
you'll get from us. If any man once vows

εὐξάμενος εἶτα διασοφίζηται λέγων,
'μενετοὶ θεοί,' καὶ μἀποδιδῷ μισητία,　　　　　　1620
ἀναπράξομεν καὶ ταῦτα.

ΠΟΣΕΙΔΩΝ

　　　　　φέρ᾽ ἴδω τῷ τρόπῳ;

ΠΙΣΘΕΤΑΙΡΟΣ
ὅταν διαριθμῶν ἀργυρίδιον τύχῃ
ἄνθρωπος οὗτος, ἢ καθῆται λούμενος,
καταπτόμενος ἰκτῖνος ἁρπάσας λάθρᾳ
προβάτοιν δυοῖν τιμὴν ἀνοίσει τῷ θεῷ.　　　　1625

ΗΡΑΚΛΗΣ
τὸ σκῆπτρον ἀποδοῦναι πάλιν ψηφίζομαι
τούτοις ἐγώ.

ΠΟΣΕΙΔΩΝ
　　　　　καὶ τὸν Τριβαλλόν νυν ἐροῦ.

ΗΡΑΚΛΗΣ
ὁ Τριβαλλός, οἰμώζειν δοκεῖ σοι;

ΤΡΙΒΑΛΛΟΣ
　　　　　　　　　　σαυνάκα
βακταρικροῦσα.

ΗΡΑΚΛΗΣ
φησί μ᾽ εὖ λέγειν πάνυ.

ΠΟΣΕΙΔΩΝ
εἴ τοι δοκεῖ σφῷν ταῦτα, κἀμοὶ συνδοκεῖ.　　　　1630

ΗΡΑΚΛΗΣ
οὗτος, δοκεῖ δρᾶν ταῦτα τοῦ σκήπτρου πέρι.

ΠΙΣΘΕΤΑΙΡΟΣ
καὶ νὴ Δί᾽ ἕτερόν γ᾽ ἐστὶν οὗ ᾽μνήσθην ἐγώ.
τὴν μὲν γὰρ Ἥραν παραδίδωμι τῷ Διί,
τὴν δὲ Βασίλειαν τὴν κόρην γυναῖκ᾽ ἐμοὶ
ἐκδοτέον ἐστίν.　　　　　　　　　　1635

to one of the gods he'll sacrifice a beast,
then tries to talk his way out of doing it
by splitting hairs and, acting on his greed,
holds back his vow, saying "Gods are patient,"   [1620]
we'll make him pay for that as well.

POSEIDON
                              How?
    Tell us how you'd do that.

PISTHETAIROS
                        Well, at some point,
    when that man is counting up his wealth
    or sitting in his bath, some kite will fly down,
    while he's not paying attention, grab his cash,
    the value of two sheep, and carry that
    up to the god.

HERCULES
                    He gets my vote again —
    I say we give the sceptre back to them.

POSEIDON
    All right — ask the Triballian.

HERCULES *[threateningly]*
                                Hey, you —
    Triballian — want me to smack you round?

TRIBALLIAN *[afraid]*
    Oo smacka skeen dat steek?

HERCULES
                        He says it's fine —
    he agrees with me.

POSEIDON
                    Well, if it's what you want,   [1630]
    then it's all right with me.

HERCULES *[to Pisthetairos]*
    Hey, we're ready to agree to terms
    about the sceptre.

PISTHETAIROS
                    By god, there's one more thing —
    I've just remembered. I'll let Zeus keep Hera,
    but he must give me that young girl Princess.
    She's to be my wife.

ΠΟΣΕΙΔΩΝ

οὐ διαλλαγῶν ἐρᾷς.
ἀπίωμεν οἴκαδ᾽ αὖθις.

ΠΙΣΘΕΤΑΙΡΟΣ

ὀλίγον μοι μέλει.
μάγειρε τὸ κατάχυσμα χρὴ ποιεῖν γλυκύ.

ΗΡΑΚΛΗΣ

ὦ δαιμόνι᾽ ἀνθρώπων Πόσειδον ποῖ φέρει;
ἡμεῖς περὶ γυναικὸς μιᾶς πολεμήσομεν;

ΠΟΣΕΙΔΩΝ

τί δαὶ ποιῶμεν;   1640

ΗΡΑΚΛΗΣ

ὅ τι; διαλλαττώμεθα.

ΠΟΣΕΙΔΩΝ

τί δ᾽ ὠζύρ᾽; οὐκ οἶσθ᾽ ἐξαπατώμενος πάλαι;
βλάπτεις δέ τοι σὺ σαυτόν. ἢν γὰρ ἀποθάνῃ
ὁ Ζεὺς παραδοὺς τούτοισι τὴν τυραννίδα,
πένης ἔσει σύ. σοῦ γὰρ ἅπαντα γίγνεται
τὰ χρήμαθ᾽, ὅσ᾽ ἂν ὁ Ζεὺς ἀποθνῄσκων καταλίπῃ.   1645

ΠΙΣΘΕΤΑΙΡΟΣ

οἴμοι τάλας οἷόν σε περισοφίζεται.
δεῦρ᾽ ὡς ἔμ᾽ ἀποχώρησον, ἵνα τί σοι φράσω.
διαβάλλεταί σ᾽ ὁ θεῖος ὦ πόνηρε σύ.
τῶν γὰρ πατρῴων οὐδ᾽ ἀκαρῆ μέτεστί σοι
κατὰ τοὺς νόμους· νόθος γὰρ εἶ κοὐ γνήσιος.   1650

ΗΡΑΚΛΗΣ

ἐγὼ νόθος; τί λέγεις;

ΠΙΣΘΕΤΑΙΡΟΣ

σὺ μέντοι νὴ Δία
ὢν γε ξένης γυναικός. ἢ πῶς ἄν ποτε
ἐπίκληρον εἶναι τὴν Ἀθηναίαν δοκεῖς,
οὖσαν θυγατέρ᾽, ὄντων ἀδελφῶν γνησίων;

POSEIDON

                                Then you don't want
a real negotiation. Come on, let's go back home.

PISTHETAIROS

        That's up to you. Hey, cook, watch that gravy.
Make sure you make it sweet!

HERCULES

                           Hey, Poseidon,
my dear fellow, where you going? Come on,
are we going to war about a woman?

POSEIDON

        What should we do?

HERCULES

                     Do? Settle this matter.

POSEIDON

        What? You fool! Don't you see what he's doing,
how all this time he's been deceiving you?
You're ruining yourself, you know. If Zeus dies,
after giving all his sovereignty to birds,
you'll have nothing. Right now you're his heir—
you get whatever's left when Zeus departs.

PISTHETAIROS *[to Hercules]*

        Oh dear, dear—how he's trying to play with you.
Come on over here—let me tell you something.

[Pisthetairos and Hercules talk apart from the others]

        You uncles's putting one over on you,
you poor fool—because, according to the law,
you don't get the smallest piece of property
from your father's goods. You're illegitimate—   [1650]
you're a bastard.

HERCULES

                 A bastard? What do you mean?

PISTHETAIROS

        I mean just what I say. Now, your mother—
she was an alien woman. And Athena—
do you think a daughter could inherit
if she's got legal brothers?

Aristophanes

ἩΡΑΚΛΗΣ

τί δ' ἦν ὁ πατὴρ ἐμοὶ διδῷ τὰ χρήματα   1655
νοθεῖ' ἀποθνῄσκων;

ΠΙΣΘΕΤΑΙΡΟΣ

ὁ νόμος αὐτὸν οὐκ ἐᾷ.
οὗτος ὁ Ποσειδῶν πρῶτος, ὃς ἐπαίρει σε νῦν,
ἀνθέξεταί σου τῶν πατρῴων χρημάτων
φάσκων ἀδελφὸς αὐτὸς εἶναι γνήσιος.
ἐρῶ δὲ δὴ καὶ τὸν Σόλωνός σοι νόμον·   1660
'νόθῳ δὲ μὴ εἶναι ἀγχιστείαν παίδων ὄντων
γνησίων. ἐὰν δὲ παῖδες μὴ ὦσι γνήσιοι, τοῖς   1665
ἐγγυτάτω γένους μετεῖναι τῶν χρημάτων.'

ἩΡΑΚΛΗΣ

ἐμοὶ δ' ἄρ' οὐδὲν τῶν πατρῴων χρημάτων
μέτεστιν;

ΠΙΣΘΕΤΑΙΡΟΣ

οὐ μέντοι μὰ Δία. λέξον δέ μοι,
ἤδη σ' ὁ πατὴρ εἰσήγαγ' ἐς τοὺς φράτερας;

ἩΡΑΚΛΗΣ

οὐ δῆτ' ἐμέ γε. καὶ δῆτ' ἐθαύμαζον πάλαι.   1670

ΠΙΣΘΕΤΑΙΡΟΣ

τί δῆτ' ἄνω κέχηνας αἴκειαν βλέπων;
ἀλλ' ἢν μεθ' ἡμῶν ᾖς, καταστήσας σ' ἐγὼ
τύραννον ὀρνίθων παρέξω σοι γάλα.

ἩΡΑΚΛΗΣ

δίκαι' ἔμοιγε καὶ πάλαι δοκεῖς λέγειν
περὶ τῆς κόρης, κἄγωγε παραδίδωμί σοι.   1675

ΠΙΣΘΕΤΑΙΡΟΣ

τί δαὶ σὺ φῄς;

ΠΟΣΕΙΔΩΝ

τἀναντία ψηφίζομαι.

178

HERCULES *[very puzzled]*

                                    But once he dies,
couldn't my dad leave me all his property
as a bastard's share?

PISTHETAIROS

                           The law won't let him.
The first one to claim your father's property
will be Poseidon here, who's raised your hopes.
He'll claim he's your father's legal brother.
I'll read you what Solon's laws dictate —   [1660]

[Pisthetairos pulls a piece of paper out and reads]

    "If there are lawful children, then a bastard
has no rights as a close blood relative.
If there are no lawful children, the goods
go to the nearest next of kin."

HERCULES

                                         What!
I don't get anything from daddy's stuff?

PISTHETAIROS

    Not a thing, by god. So tell me this —
has your father introduced you to his kin group yet?[88]

HERCULES

    No, not me. As a matter of fact,
I've been wondering about that for some time.

PISTHETAIROS

    Well, don't just stare up there, mouth wide open,
planning an assault. Join up with us instead.
I'll make you a king and give you bird's milk.

HERCULES

    I've always thought you're right in what you say
about the girl. I'd hand her over to you.

PISTHETAIROS *[to Poseidon]*

    What do you say?

POSEIDON

                       I vote no.

Aristophanes

ΠΙΣΘΕΤΑΙΡΟΣ
ἐν τῷ Τριβαλλῷ πᾶν τὸ πρᾶγμα. τί σὺ λέγεις;

ΤΡΙΒΑΛΛΟΣ
καλάνι κόραυνα καὶ μεγάλα βασιλιναῦ
ὄρνιτο παραδίδωμι.

ΗΡΑΚΛΗΣ
παραδοῦναι λέγει.

ΠΟΣΕΙΔΩΝ
μὰ τὸν Δί᾽ οὐχ οὗτός γε παραδοῦναι λέγει,   1680
εἰ μὴ † βαδίζειν † ὥσπερ αἱ χελιδόσιν λέγει.

ΗΡΑΚΛΗΣ
οὐκοῦν παραδοῦναι ταῖς χελιδόσιν λέγει.

ΠΟΣΕΙΔΩΝ
σφὼ νῦν διαλλάττεσθε καὶ ξυμβαίνετε·
ἐγὼ δ᾽, ἐπειδὴ σφῷν δοκεῖ, σιγήσομαι.

ΗΡΑΚΛΗΣ
ἡμῖν ἃ λέγεις σὺ πάντα συγχωρεῖν δοκεῖ.   1685
ἀλλ᾽ ἴθι μεθ᾽ ἡμῶν αὐτὸς ἐς τὸν οὐρανόν,
ἵνα τὴν Βασίλειαν καὶ τὰ πάντ᾽ ἐκεῖ λάβῃς.

ΠΙΣΘΕΤΑΙΡΟΣ
ἐς καιρὸν ἆρα κατεκόπησαν οὑτοιὶ
ἐς τοὺς γάμους.

ΗΡΑΚΛΗΣ
βούλεσθε δῆτ᾽ ἐγὼ τέως
ὀπτῶ τὰ κρέα ταυτὶ μένων; ὑμεῖς δ᾽ ἴτε.   1690

ΠΟΣΕΙΔΩΝ
ὀπτᾷς τὰ κρέα; πολλήν γε τενθείαν λέγεις.
οὐκ εἶ μεθ᾽ ἡμῶν;

ΗΡΑΚΛΗΣ
εὖ γε μέντἂν διετέθην.

ΠΙΣΘΕΤΑΙΡΟΣ
ἀλλὰ γαμικὴν χλανίδα δότω τις δεῦρό μοι.

180

PISTHETAIROS

                                 So now,
it's up to the Triballian here. What you say?

TRIBALLIAN

    De geerl geeve over greet souvrin bridies.

HERCULES

    There! He says to hand her over.

POSEIDON

                              No by god!   [1680]
he never said to give her up — no way.
He's just babbling like a swallow.

HERCULES

    So he said hand her over to the swallows!

POSEIDON

    You two work it out — agree on peace terms.
Since you're both for it, I'll say nothing more.

HERCULES

    We ready now to give you all you ask.
So come along with us in person —
up to heaven — there you can get your Princess,
and all those other things as well.

PISTHETAIROS *[pointing to the cooking he's been preparing]*
    So these birds were slaughtered in good time
before the wedding feast.

HERCULES

                          If you want to,
I could stay here and roast the meat. You go.   [1690]

POSEIDON

    Roast the meat? You mean you'd wolf it down,
you glutton. Come on with us. Let's go.

HERCULES *[reluctantly leaving]*
    I'd have enjoyed eating that.

PISTHETAIROS *[calling to his slaves]*
                           Hey, you —
one of you bring me out some wedding clothes!

ΧΟΡΟΣ

ἔστι δ᾽ ἐν Φαναῖσι πρὸς τῇ
   Κλεψύδρᾳ πανοῦργον ἐγ-   1695
   γλωττογαστόρων γένος,
οἳ θερίζουσίν τε καὶ σπείρουσι
καὶ τρυγῶσι ταῖς γλώτταισι
   συκάζουσί τε·
βάρβαροι δ᾽ εἰσὶν γένος,   1700
Γοργίαι τε καὶ Φίλιπποι.
κἀπὸ τῶν ἐγγλωττογαστόρων
ἐκείνων τῶν Φιλίππων
πανταχοῦ τῆς Ἀττικῆς ἡ
   γλῶττα χωρὶς τέμνεται.   1705

ἌΓΓΕΛΟΣ Β

ὦ πάντ᾽ ἀγαθὰ πράττοντες, ὦ μείζω λόγου,
ὦ τρισμακάριον πτηνὸν ὀρνίθων γένος,
δέχεσθε τὸν τύραννον ὀλβίοις δόμοις.
προσέρχεται γὰρ οἷς οὔτε παμφαὴς
ἀστὴρ ἰδεῖν ἔλαμψε χρυσαυγεῖ δόμῳ,   1710
οὔθ᾽ ἡλίου τηλαυγὲς ἀκτίνων σέλας
τοιοῦτον ἐξέλαμψεν, οἷον ἔρχεται
ἔχων γυναικὸς κάλλος οὐ φατὸν λέγειν,
πάλλων κεραυνόν, πτεροφόρον Διὸς βέλος·
ὀσμὴ δ᾽ ἀνωνόμαστος ἐς βάθος κύκλου   1715
χωρεῖ, καλὸν θέαμα· θυμιαμάτων δ᾽
αὖραι διαψαίρουσι πλεκτάνην καπνοῦ.
ὁδὶ δὲ καὐτός ἐστιν. ἀλλὰ χρὴ θεᾶς
Μούσης ἀνοίγειν ἱερὸν εὔφημον στόμα.

ΧΟΡΟΣ

ἄναγε δίεχε πάραγε πάρεχε.   1720
   περιπέτεσθε
τὸν μάκαρα μάκαρι σὺν τύχᾳ.
ὦ φεῦ φεῦ τῆς ὥρας τοῦ κάλλους.
ὦ μακαριστὸν σὺ γάμον τῇδε πόλει γήμας.   1725

CHORUS
>In lands of Litigation there's a place—
>it's right beside the water clock—
>where that villainous and thieving race
>of tongue-and-belly men all flock.
>They use their tongues to sow and reap,
>to harvest grapes and figs en masse.
>A crude barbarian tribe, a heap   [1700]
>of Philipses and Gorgias.
>From these horse-loving sycophants,
>who use their tongues to cram their gut,
>through all of Attica's expanse
>in sacrifice the tongue's first cut.[89]

[Enter Second Herald]

SECOND HERALD
>You here who've done fine things, more wonderful
>than I can say, you thrice-blessed race with wings,
>you birds, welcome now your king on his return,
>as he comes back among these wealthy halls.
>Here he approaches—you'll never see a star
>so bright in any gleaming home of gold.   [1710]
>No—not even the far-reaching rays of sun
>have ever shone as splendidly as he,
>the man who brings with him his lovely wife,
>too beautiful for words, and brandishing
>the winged thunderbolt from Zeus. Sweet smells
>are rising up, high into heaven's vault,
>a glorious spectacle, and wisps of smoke
>from burning incense are blown far and wide.
>Here he is in person. Let the sacred Muse
>open her lips in a triumphal holy song.

[Enter Pisthetairos and his bride Princess]

CHORUS
>Back off, break up, make room—   [1720]
>And wing your way around the man
>so blessed with blissful fortune.
>Oh, oh—such beauty and such youth!
>What a blessing for this city of the birds
>is this fine marriage you have made.

Aristophanes

μεγάλαι μεγάλαι κατέχουσι τύχαι
γένος ὀρνίθων
διὰ τόνδε τὸν ἄνδρ'. ἀλλ' ὑμεναίοις
καὶ νυμφιδίοισι δέχεσθ' ᾠδαῖς
αὐτὸν καὶ τὴν Βασίλειαν.   1730

Ἥρᾳ ποτ' Ὀλυμπίᾳ
τῶν ἠλιβάτων θρόνων
ἄρχοντα θεοῖς μέγαν
Μοῖραι ξυνεκοίμισαν
ἐν τοιῷδ' ὑμεναίῳ.   1735
Ὑμὴν ὦ Ὑμέναι' ὦ,
Ὑμὴν ὦ Ὑμέναι' ὦ.

ὁ δ' ἀμφιθαλὴς Ἔρως
χρυσόπτερος ἡνίας
ηὔθυνε παλιντόνους,
Ζηνὸς πάροχος γάμων   1740
τῆς τ' εὐδαίμονος Ἥρας.
Ὑμὴν ὦ Ὑμέναι' ὦ,
Ὑμὴν ὦ Ὑμέναι' ὦ.

ΠΙΣΘΕΤΑΙΡΟΣ
ἐχάρην ὕμνοις, ἐχάρην ᾠδαῖς·
ἄγαμαι δὲ λόγων.

ΧΟΡΟΣ
ἄγε νυν αὐτοῦ καὶ τὰς χθονίας   1745
κλῄσατε βροντὰς τάς τε πυρώδεις
Διὸς ἀστεροπὰς
δεινόν τ' ἀργῆτα κεραυνόν.

ὦ μέγα χρύσεον ἀστεροπῆς φάος,
ὦ Διὸς ἄμβροτον ἔγχος πυρφόρον,
ὦ χθόνιαι βαρυαχέες   1750
ὀμβροφόροι θ' ἅμα βρονταί,
αἷς ὅδε νῦν χθόνα σείει.
διὰ σὲ τὰ πάντα κρατήσας
καὶ πάρεδρον Βασίλειαν ἔχει Διός.
Ὑμὴν ὦ Ὑμέναι' ὦ.

184

A great good fortune now attends us,
the race of birds—such mighty bliss,
thanks to this man. So welcome back
with nuptial chants and wedding songs
our man himself and his Princess.

Olympian Hera and great Zeus
who rules the gods on lofty thrones
the Fates once joined with wedding songs.
O Hymen, Hymenaeus⁹⁰

And rich young Eros in his golden wings
held tight the reins as charioteer
at Zeus' wedding to the happy Hera.

O Hymen, Hymenaeus,
O Hymen, Hymenaeus.

PISTHETAIROS

    Your chants fill me with great delight,
    as do you songs. And I just love your words.

CHORUS

    Come now, celebrate in song
    earth-shattering thunder, Zeus' lightning fire—
    which now belong to him—
    that dreaded bolt white lighting, too.
    Oh, that great golden blaze of lightning,
    that immortal fiery spear of Zeus,
    and groaning thunders bringing rain—   [1750]
    with you this man now rattles Earth.
    And everything that Zeus once had,
    he's got it all—and that includes
    our Princess, who once sat by Zeus' throne.
    O Hymen, Hymenaeus!

Aristophanes

ΠΙΣΘΕΤΑΙΡΟΣ

ἕπεσθε νῦν γάμοισιν ὦ   1755
φῦλα πάντα συννόμων
πτεροφόρ' ἐπὶ δάπεδον Διὸς
καὶ λέχος γαμήλιον.
ὄρεξον ὦ μάκαιρα σὴν
χεῖρα καὶ πτερῶν ἐμῶν   1760
λαβοῦσα συγχόρευσον· αἴρων
δὲ κουφιῶ σ' ἐγώ.

ΧΟΡΟΣ

ἀλαλαλαὶ ἰὴ παιών,
τήνελλα καλλίνικος, ὦ
δαιμόνων ὑπέρτατε.   1765

186

PISTHETAIROS

> Now all you feathered tribes of friends,
> come follow me on this my wedding flight.
> Let's wing our way up there to Zeus' house
> and to our wedding bed. Reach out your hand,
> my blissful love, and take hold of my wing—   [1760]
> then dance with me. I'll lift and carry you.

[Pisthetairos and Princess lead the procession off the stage]

CHORUS

> Alalalalai—
> Raise triumphal cries of joy,
> sing out the noble victor's song—
> the mightiest and highest of all gods!

[The procession exits singing and dancing, accompanying Pisthetairos and his bride up to Heaven]

NOTES

1   *Execestides*: An Athenian descended from Carian slaves and therefore not entitled to be a citizen. The point here is that he must have been extremely skilful to get to Athens, given where he started, and even he couldn't navigate his way back to Athens in this terrain.

2   *Tereus*: the name of a mythological king of Thrace who married Procne and raped her sister Philomela. The sisters killed his son and fed Tereus the flesh for dinner. All three were changed into birds: Tereus into a hoopoe, Procne into a nightingale, and Philomela into a swallow.

3   *Tharreleides*: the reference here seems to be to a well-known member of the audience, perhaps celebrated for his small size and loud voice.

4   *birds*: the Greek expression is "to the Ravens," meaning "go to hell."

5   *Sacas*: a name for Acestor, a foreign-born tragic dramatist.

6   *tribe and clan*: the political units of Athenian civic life.

7   *basket, pot, and myrtle boughs*: these materials were necessary to conduct the sacrifices at the founding of a new city.

8   *twelve gods*: the major Olympian deities, headed by Zeus.

9   Most Athenians knew very little about peacocks.

10   *Cranaus*: reference to a mythological king who founded Athens or a word derived from *kranaos*, meaning rugged, a word often applied to Athens.

11   *son of Scellias*: the reference is to a man called Aristocrates, an important politician-soldier in Athens.

12   *difficult for me*: this is a utopian fantasy because the neighbour is suggesting that, as a punishment, his friend Euelpides would not have to help him if he gets in financial trouble, even though he's invited him to an important family celebration.

13   *Red Sea*: a general term for any sea by the southern coasts of Asia.

14 *summons*: Athenian citizens could be legally summoned home for trial. Salamia was an official ship often used for such voyages.

15 *Melanthius' fault*: the reference is to an Athenian tragic dramatist who had a very bad skin condition (making him look as if he had leprosy).

16 *Opuntius*: a widely disliked Athenian informer. A talent's weight is just under 30 kilograms.

17 *Teleus*: Athenian politician with a reputation for being unpredictable.

18 *Melos*: the Athenians committed a horrible atrocity during the Peloponnesian War, starving the population of Melos and then executing all male citizens.

19 In some productions of *The Birds* the set design permits the audience to see inside Tereus' quarters, so that the singer of the songs which follow remains visible to the audience. Alternatively, Tereus could move out onto a rocky balcony to deliver his song. It seems dramatically very weak to have him deliver these lyrics out of sight of the audience.

20 *Itys*: son of Tereus and Procne, killed by his mother, who served him up as dinner, in revenge for Tereus' rape and mutilation of her sister.

21 *Hipponicus*: this passages refers to the Greek custom of naming children after their grandfathers. Philocles was a tragic dramatist. Callias, his son, was a notorious spendthrift who squandered his family inheritance on a debauched lifestyle.

22 *Cleonymus*: an Athenian politician well known for his eating habits and his size. He also reputedly once threw his shield away in battle and ran off.

23 *safer*: Pisthetairos refers to a race in which the runners wore helmets with plumes (crests), but Tereus misunderstands and talks about mountain crests where the birds live. Caria is in Asia Minor.

24 *shaver*: the Greek bird *kerulos* was a mythological species. The passage here plays on the similarity of the verb *keirein* meaning to cut hair.

25 *Athens*: to bring owls to Athens is an expression for something totally unnecessary (like bringing coals to Newcastle).

26 *Nikias*: Athenian general famous for his tactical skill.

27 *Orneai*: a siege in which some Athenians took part. There were no casualties.

28 *win*: a reference to the fact that *The Birds* is competing in a drama festival.

29 *Earth*: Kronos was the father of Zeus; the Titans were the sons of Kronos. Earth was the original mother goddess.

30 *Halimus*: a community on the coast near Athens.

31 *kite*: an old Greek custom of saluting the kite as the bird announcing the arrival of spring by rolling on the ground. This speech refers to the habit of carrying small coins in the mouth. Having eaten his money, he can't buy the food he set out to purchase.

32 These lines are an attempt to deal with an totally obscure sexual pun in the Greek.

33 *Lysicrates gets*: a reference to a corrupt Athenian politician.

34 *Lampon*: a well known soothsayer in Athens. "By Goose" is a euphemistic way of swearing "By Zeus."

35 *Kebriones* and *Porphyrion* were two Giants who fought against the Olympian gods.

36 These women all had sexual encounters with gods. Alkmeneand Zeus produced Hercules; Semele and Zeus produced Dionysus; and Alope and Poseidon produced Hippothoon.

37 *Zan*: an archaic and contemptuous name for Zeus.

38 *crow*: in legend and folk lore the life span of the crow was enormous.

39 *Nikias*: Athenian general, famous for his hesitation about tactics.

40 *Erebus*: the primeval darkness.

41 *Prodicus*: a reference to a well known philosopher who offered a materialistic explanation for the origin of the gods.

42 These lines refer to the custom of giving one's lover a bird as a present.

43 *Orestes*: the reference is to a well-known thief of other people's

clothing.

44   In other words, we're all the oracles you need. Ammon, Delphi, and Dodona are shrines famous for prophecy. Apollo is the god of prophecy.

45   *Diitrephes*: prominent Athenian politician and general. A horse-cock is a mythological animal with the front of a horse and the rear of a cock.

46   poor people used esparto grass to make rope chords to hold up the mattress. Rich folks used linen. The pun here is obviously on Sparta-esparto. Euelpides won't have anything to do with Sparta or anything that sounds like it.

47   *Theogenes and Aeschines*: two Athenian business men who constantly boasted they were richer than they were.

48   the *giants* were the monstrous children of Uranus; the gods are the Olympians, headed by Zeus. The point here is thatCloudcuckooland is so great, it's a place for divine boasting, not just the sort of thing rich Athenians might brag about.

49   *Cleisthenes*: a well-known homosexual in Athens, often satirized by Aristophanes.

50   The officer inspecting the sentries regularly rang a small bell to indicate that all was well.

51   *Hestia*: traditional goddess of the hearth.

52   *Cleocritus*: a very ugly Athenian who was often compared to an ostrich.

53   The *Chians* were staunch allies of Athens in the Peloponnesian War.

54   *Simonides*: well-known lyric poet of the previous generation.

55   These lines are a jumble of allusions to well known poems. The founder of Aetna is Heiron, ruler of Syracuse, whose name is the same as the word for "of holy things." In Homer a nod of the head signifies divine assent.

56   *Lampon and Diopeithes* were well-known soothsayers in Athens.

57   *Meton* was a famous astronomer and engineer.

58   *Colonus*: a district of Athens.

59   *Thales*: very famous astronomer and thinker from distant past. Thales is often considered the founder of philosophy.

60   *Commissioner*: an official who was sent out to supervise and report on a new colony.

61   *Sardanapallos* was the last king of Assyria, famous in legend for his extravagant lifestyle and appearance.

62   *Teleas*, an Athenian politician, would have proposed sending the Commissioner out.

63   *Pharnakes* was an important Persian official. Dealing with him would be considered treasonous in some quarters.

64   A small town in the remote north east of Greece (by Mount Athos).

65   At the drama festival formal public announcements like this were part of the script. Diagoras was a notorious atheist who had fled Athens. The reward for killing old tyrants was part of a ritual pronouncement to protect democracy.

66   *Alexander*: another name for Paris of Troy.

67   The owls of Laureium are coins. The owl was stamped on Athenian coins, and Laureium was the site of the silver mines.

68   Greek temples commonly had triangular pediments known as "eagles."

69   Pisthetairus compares Iris to a ship because her dressing is billowing like a sail. The two names he gives are the two main flag ships of the Athenian fleet.

70   *Porphyrion* was the name of one of the giants who went to war against Zeus.

71   The lines following refer to a number of political figures in Athens.

72   This reference is to a very popular betting game in which a quail was placed inside a circle and tapped on the head to see if it would back off or stand its ground.

73   Manes is probably another name for Manodoros, since there are only two slaves in the play.

74 I follow Sommerstein's useful suggestion and add this line here to make sense of the lines which follow.

75 At the festival for tragic drama, the war orphans were paraded around in special armour given to them by the state.

76 *Cinesias* was a well-known and frequently satirized poet in Athens. He was extremely thin and evidently suffered very badly from diarrhea.

77 The tribes were the political divisions in Athenian life. The dithyrambic competitions were organized by tribes, each one wanting the services of the best poets.

78 *Leotrophides* was another Athenian famous for being extremely thin (like Cinesias).

79 The point here seems to be that the Sycophant's cloak is so thin and worn that he's singing for warm weather, when he won't need it.

80 Cranes reputedly swallowed stones to serve as ballast on their flights.

81 These lines refer to the notion that meeting up with ghosts of heroes is all right during the day but harmful at night. There is also another reference here to the thief Orestes (mentioned earlier by the Chorus Leader) who beats people and steals their clothes.

82 *Thesmophoria*: an important religious festival in Greece, during which there was a period of fasting.

83 *Triballians*: the name of a barbarian tribe in Thrace, north of Greece. The Tiballian god who enters with Poseidon and Hercules a few lines later on cannot speak Greek, so his lines are incomprehensible gibberish.

84 *Prometheus* stole fire from heaven and gave it to human beings.

85 *Timon* was a legendary Athenian who hated his fellow citizens.

86 *Peisander*: an Athenian with a reputation for corruption and cowardice. Chaerephon was well known as an associate of Socrates.

87 *Laespodias*: Athenian politician who dressed oddly to conceal his misshapen legs.

88 A kin group (*phrateres*) was a group of citizens who shared a common ancestor.

89 These lines attack the Sophists who earned their living by teaching rhetoric. Gorgias was a famous sophist and Philip was his pupil and disciple. They are called horse-loving either to suggest extravagant ambitions or their non-Athenian tribal origins. In sacrificing an animal, the Athenians cut out the tongue first. The suggestion seems to be that that's what the speaker would like to do with the Sophists.

90 A customary salute to the gods of marriage.

Made in the USA
Middletown, DE
25 June 2021